T5-AXI-458

Brooks & Dunn
The Honky Tonk Truth

Text by M.B. Roberts
Photography by Ronald C. Modra

W.C. Books

Minocqua, Wisconsin

Brooks & Dunn
The Honky Tonk Truth

© 2001 M.B. Roberts and Ronald C. Modra

Published by W.C. Books
an imprint of Willow Creek Press
P.O. Box 147
Minocqua, WI 54548

All rights reserved. No part of this book may be reproduced or
transmitted in any form by any means, electronic or mechanical,
including photocopying, recording, or by any information storage
and retrieval system, without permission in writing from the publisher.

Cover and book design by R. S. K. Book Design

Library of Congress Cataloging-in-Publication Data
Roberts, M. B. (Mary Beth)
  Brooks & Dunn : the honky tonk truth / text by M.B. Roberts ;
photography by Ronald C. Modra.
    p. cm.
  ISBN 1-57223-216-1 (softcover : alk. paper)
  1. Brooks & Dunn (Musical group) 2. Country musicians--United
States--Biography. 1. Title: Brooks and Dunn. II. Modra, Ronald C. III.
Title.
  ML421.B76 R63 2001
  782.421642'092'2--dc21
                                    2001000763

Printed in Canada

Table of Contents

PREFACE 6

FOREWORD BY DALE EARNHARDT 9

INTRODUCTION 10

CHAPTER 1
BROOKS . . . AND DUNN 17

CHAPTER 2
THE ONE WITH THE HAT 37

CHAPTER 3
THE TALL ONE WITH THE BEARD . . . 63

CHAPTER 4
ROAD DOGS 89

CHAPTER 5
HILLBILLY SONGS 117

CHAPTER 6
THIS BROOKS & DUNN THING 141

Preface

It was late one night in the summer of 1993. My husband, Ron Modra, who has been a *Sports Illustrated* contract photographer since 1978, called me from Atlanta after he finished working at a Braves game.

"You'll never guess who I met," he said.
"Who?" I yawned.
"Ronnie Dunn!"
"Who?" I yawned again.
"Ronnie Dunn!" he said. "You know, from *Brooks & Dunn*! Boot Scootin' Boogie..."

Oh yeah. The guys from the record Ron had been cranking at every recent backyard barbeque. They were pretty good, I thought. And I wasn't even much of a country music fan.

Ron continued: mutual friend Ned Yost, then the Braves' bullpen coach, introduced them. Then Dunn told him, "Man, we need some good photography. Would you be interested in taking some shots at one of our shows?"

Enter my "inner Yoko Ono."

"How much they paying?" I asked.

Ron said he didn't know. And he didn't care. A man could only photograph so many baseball games in his lifetime. This sounded like fun.

Ron photographed several concerts that year. Then, in the summer of 1994, Ron and I went to The Minnesota State Fair so he could photograph *Brooks & Dunn* performing on the gigantic outdoor stage. We arrived early and found our way backstage. I camped out in the press room, planning to stay out of the way. This was my usual m.o. when accompanying him on assignments.

People think it's glamorous to hang out in dugouts or near locker rooms, but I almost always feel uncomfortable. I often find the sports scene intimidating. The *Brooks & Dunn* crew was different though. First came tour manager Scott Edwards. He poked his head into the empty room where I was sitting. "Y'all want some chicken?" he asked. "C'mon. I'll show you where it is."

As I walked down the hallway towards the chicken buffet, media coordinator, Doug Nichols, stopped and said, "Hi. You doing okay?" What I immediately noticed was that he actually waited around for my response.

I went outside to join Ron who was sitting on a picnic bench. Lead guitarist Charlie Crowe approached us warmly with an outstretched hand. He sat down and talked with us for almost an hour, asking us questions about ourselves. Folks from the South or small towns in the Midwest may not find this out of the ordinary. But during Ron's last assignment, a feature with the Cleveland Indians, I spent the afternoon dodging balls which were purposely chucked in my direction by players taking batting practice. This "friendly thing" was new.

Two guys came along riding bikes around the track behind the stage. Ron introduced me to Kix Brooks and producer Don Cook who stopped to talk with us. Kix couldn't have looked more relaxed if he was sitting in a hot tub holding a margarita. I kept thinking, "Doesn't he have a show to do?"

A half an hour later, we were standing on the track waiting for Ronnie and Kix to drive by in a golf cart on their way to a "Meet and Greet" in a V.I.P. tent on the lawn. Ron wanted to get a picture of them driving by. All at once they came zooming out of a garage, Ronnie Dunn behind the wheel. The Country Music Association's Best Duo giggled like kids as Ronnie zigged and zagged the golf cart along the track. Then Ronnie noticed us and motored over. "Well, hey," he said. We chatted for a few minutes until Doug Nichols came jogging up to nudge them along.

"I'm so glad you're here," Ronnie called over his shoulder as he drove towards the tent.

We were sitting backstage waiting for the opening act, Pam Tillis, to start. Again, I was in mind-my-own-business mode when production manager, Randy "Baja" Fletcher, took me by the elbow.

"Want to go out front and see the show?" he asked.

"O.K.," I muttered.

Baja, a big teddy-bear of a guy with a huge, red-cheeked smile, led me through a maze of technicians, security guys and fans, and planted me in the audience, front and center. It was great, but as Pam's set finished, I wondered how I'd ever get backstage again. Then, here came Baja, flashlight in hand, motioning me back.

"Thought you might want to get a Coke before the guys go on," he smiled.

That was the first time I met the *Brooks & Dunn* bunch, and my impressions still stand: friendly, helpful, and as down-home as country music is supposed to be.

Not long after, Ron and I began work on this book. We were constantly amazed by the hospitality we were offered by people in this organization.

When we went out on the Brooks & Dunn/Reba tour, fiddle player Jimmy Stewart and steel guitar player, Troy Klontz, seemed to adopt us. They took me rollerblading; sat with us at dinner. Angels in the bodies of men.

We bonded with drummer Dony Wynn one night in Jacksonville. Our fates were sealed as we linked arms and made our way across the grassy field that stood between the pub we'd just closed and our hotel. We both hope this talented man will long be our friend.

I appreciate bass player, Danny Milliner, for his intensity, deep intellect, and incredible sense of humor. And I simply appreciate keyboardist Dwain Rowe, guitarist/back-up singer Tony King and drummer Scotty Hawkins. Can these three ever be caught without a smile? And Charlie Crowe, the first one we got to know, and his sweet wife, Kim — betcha didn't know we were gonna move in!

We wouldn't have known where to begin without Melanie Robertson, who was our woman on the ground at Brooks & Dunn, Inc. We counted on her always, but the best part was just being with her and her awesome husband, Rob Hajacos.

One of the benefits of doing this book was getting to meet Kathy and Terry McBride. Terry not only writes #1 songs, he is my nomination for the funniest man alive.

We appreciate the hospitality of the crew, especially Jeff Kersey, Hud Haney, Keith Anderson, John Marsh and Larry Boster. And we appreciate all the help from everyone at Titley Spalding, especially Brenna Davenport-Leigh, Clarence Spalding, Bob Titley, and everyone at B&D, Inc., especially Terri Miller and Tricia Bullard. Thanks also to our Arista connections, Maude Gillman and Allen Brown. And to all the studio musicians, especially Brent Mason, thank you.

Special thanks to Dale Earnhardt for the foreword (and to Marie Lucas and Judy Queen for getting it done!).

Most of all we have to thank Kix Brooks and Ronnie Dunn for giving us the chance to work on this book with them. Their families welcomed us into their homes. Barbara Brooks took us horseback riding. Janine Dunn invited us to ride on their bus. They let us intrude on their infrequent private time and we appreciate it.

It is often said that "unauthorized" books are better than books done with subjects' cooperation. I've seen instances where this is true. But to provide a fan or reader with behind-the-scenes material, an author or photographer has to be behind-the-scenes. We are grateful that this extremely down-to-earth duo, and everybody around them, let us be the proverbial bugs on the wall.

Also, thanks to everyone at Willow Creek Press, especially the die-hard B&D fans in the bunch. And thanks to our guru, our man, John Passariello, for keeping the ship afloat. Finally, we'd like to remember our dear friend, Tommy Burns. You are the best boot-scooter there ever was. You'll be with us forever.

MB Roberts & Ron Modra

In Loving Memory

Dale Earnhardt   1951-2001

Just days before this book went to press in February 2001, our dear friend Dale Earnhardt died in a tragic accident while competing in the Daytona 500. There are no words to describe the loss of this great man who we were fortunate enough to know as a true friend.

We would like to dedicate this book to his memory and incredible spirit.

Kix Brooks   Ronnie Dunn

Foreword

by Dale Earnhardt

I've been fortunate in my chosen profession, in that I've been extremely successful. The fame and fortune that I've been blessed with has opened a lot of doors for me that I never would have been able to step through otherwise.

I've met U.S. Presidents, dozens of actors, artists, scholars, writers, craftsmen and yes, musicians.

I don't specifically recall where or when it was that I met Kix Brooks and Ronnie Dunn, but I remember that they both made a favorable impression on me. Our initial meeting may have been at the track, more than likely at driver introductions or something like that.

Music is a big part of our lives and I'm a country music fan. But mostly, I'm a big fan of my friends, and that's basically what Kix Brooks and Ronnie Dunn have evolved into, friends. From the first time we met, there was something more than just "hi." From the beginning, the friendship was genuine.

Kix and Ronnie are two unique individuals who complement each other. That's why they're so good. They are genuine performers who are not only sincere in their work, but also sincere in being true friends and honest people. I can relate and I think the fans relate with them because they are real and down-to-earth.

They're great guys who have become so notable and famous, I think, because they're original. They've paid their dues and deserve what they've accomplished. As our paths crossed more and more, I began to realize that the three of us were more alike, both professionally and personally, than I ever imagined.

We share a common dedication to what we do. I strive to get every tenth of a second from a racecar and they strive to make sure every note is in perfect harmony with all of the others. Like myself, they're not happy unless everything is just right. When they're performing, they're giving 110 percent. As a result, Brooks and Dunn are one of the most highly regarded duos in music today. I have the highest respect for their dedication as professionals and to this day I enjoy their music as much as I did the first time I heard it.

I've been very fortunate to know them personally and to see how real and down-to-earth they truly are. One aspect of knowing Kix and Ronnie personally is relating to the common traits we share. We think along the same lines when it comes to our personal lives—family and friends come first. If at times that means putting career goals on hold, then so be it. We like life simple and we like time to ourselves to enjoy what's going on around us.

Sometimes things happen so fast, you don't know what you've missed until it's too late. I'm just glad that I have friends like Kix and Ronnie whose music reminds us to slow down once in a while.

I am fortunate that we are good friends. Whether you're winning or losing, they will take you like you are. It isn't about I drive racecars and they play music, but when they do play music, I listen. I'm proud of them and it's great to see these guys do what they do.

Dale Earnhardt, November 2000

"They were doing the time trials for the Brickyard 400, and we were doing a show in Indianapolis. As soon as it opened, we hiked through the crowd to see Earnhardt. I was carrying a box of Wheaties that had him on the cover and I wanted the greatest race car driver to ever live sign my box."

—Ronnie

Introduction

"O.K...which is Brooks & which is Dunn?"   —*David Letterman*

It's a hot and humid July day in New Orleans. *Brooks & Dunn* is in town for a show at the Coliseum. It's noon and the show is hours away. Ronnie Dunn is having lunch with his family and some friends at Johnny Po' Boys in the French Quarter. From the corner of one eye, he sees a guy approaching his table. The guy has his eyes locked on Ronnie, trying desperately to make eye contact.

Ronnie pretends not to notice. The guy then plants himself right in front of him and bursts into a huge grin. Ronnie puts down his glass and politely nods at the guy who points at him and says, "Kix Brooks, right?"

Ronnie smiles and nods again. The friend sitting next to Ronnie looks at the guy and says, "But he's..."

Ronnie cuts her off, whispering, "Let him go. Just let him go..."

Later that night at the Coliseum, about 30 minutes prior to showtime, two forty-something women are standing in the back of a line to buy *Brooks & Dunn* T-shirts, programs and hats. The women are both wearing black *Brooks & Dunn* T-shirts from a previous tour. They look like excited teenagers, elbowing each other and giggling.

"We're big fans," one of the women says.

"Oh, definitely!" squeals her friend, "I just love that Ronnie Brooks and his tight pants."

Ten minutes to showtime. Down on the floor, just 10 rows back from the stage, a fortyish guy with a black mustache, wearing a black cowboy hat and the Panhandle Slim button-down flame shirt that Kix Brooks made famous, is milling around talking to some fans. The guy is a dead ringer for Kix.

"Hi!" says the lookalike. "My name is Bruce LeBlanc. Everybody tells me I look like *Brooks & Dunn*."

ORIGINAL
OLD ABSINTHE BAR
Est. 1806

A tradition in the french quarters. This is the
bar known to travelers the world over. From it
came the famous absinthe drip. The Bar where
Jean & Pierre LaFitte, Andrew Jackson,
Mark Twain and other celebrities were served.
If it could talk what stories the Bar would tell
of a thousand & one nights crowded into history.

It's Fall, 1998 in Tombstone, Arizona. A wannabe movie cowboy sits in Big Nose Kate's bar drinking a beer. The cowboy is talking to a photographer who will be working on the set of Brooks & Dunn's "South of Santa Fe" video, which will be shot the next day.

"Oh!" says the cowboy. "I tried out for that! They didn't pick me, but I can tell you the whole story. Now Dunn is a bad guy. Brooks is chasing Dunn with his posse. Dunn get shot and dies..."

The photographer looks at his companion. "That's backwards, right? *Kix* dies in the video..."

His companion nods yes, but the cowboy insists and continues with his story.

It's Sunday afternoon. Kix Brooks is standing in his driveway, unloading a suitcase from his car. A minivan pulls into the long, uphill driveway. "Excuse me?" the driver says, rolling down his window. "Don't they live around here?"

"Come again?" Kix says, putting down the suitcase.

"You know, Brooks & Dunn," the man says. "Don't they live around here?"

"I heard one of them does," Kix says. "Try Stuart Street. Three blocks down."

Imagine it's the late seventies. Ronnie Dunn is singing in a dark Texas honky-tonk. A chicken-wire curtain separates his band from the beer bottle-chucking patrons. They're playing for the door. He and the band leave that night with $11 each, which they pocket after hauling their own gear off the stage and loading it into Ronnie's Mercury Capri.

About 300 miles away on Bourbon Street in New Orleans, Kix Brooks is sitting in the doorway of The Old Absinthe House singing to bar patrons and fending off hecklers walking by on the street. Kix plays all night and into the wee hours for a small fee plus tips.

What if after the night's performance, the devil himself made a trip to Texas, then to New Orleans, and appeared to Ronnie and Kix. What if he said to each of them, separately, since they had never met, *Have I got a deal for you...You can be a star. You can have your dream. But you have to share. People will sometimes think you are one thing. Or they might even confuse you for him. They might think you live together. I'll give you what you want, but it comes with...him.*

What would they have said?

Hell, yeah.

It took over ten years. But the devil finally showed up.

*"When they met, neither Ronnie or Kix
were music neophytes . . ."*
—Tim DuBois

BROOKS . . . AND DUNN

TIM DUBOIS had more than a burrito in mind one day in October of 1990 when he asked Ronnie Dunn and Kix Brooks, who had not met each other yet, to have lunch with him in Nashville. DuBois, the new president of Arista Records' Nashville division, was assembling artists for his label. He had Alan Jackson, Diamond Rio, and Pam Tillis, but there was a gaping hole: he didn't have a duo.

And he wanted one. But he didn't tell Ronnie and Kix that. He just asked them to lunch.

"It was this little, bitty Mexican food hole-in-the-wall," Ronnie says. "One of those squirt-cheese joints. You had to get up and get it. Everything came out of a microwave on Styrofoam plates."

The casual setting allowed DuBois to underplay his proposal that Ronnie and Kix try "working together." Like a woman suggesting her girlfriend drop by at the same time her single brother happens to be visiting, DuBois was up to something. But he kept things low-key.

"We were both trying to get a solo deal," Kix says, "so we'd do anything to pacify Tim in hopes that we'd get our way in the end."

Prior to their blind date, DuBois had played Kix's song, "Lost and Found," for Ronnie.

"At the time it was pretty progressive." Ronnie says. "It had a little bit of that California-cowboy, Eagles kind of deal. I said it was cool."

DuBois also played Ronnie's song, "Neon Moon," for Kix, who says he remembers thinking, "Shoot. The guy's a good writer and he's a damn good singer."

*"Where did an Okie learn
a word like 'neophyte'?"*
—Kix Brooks

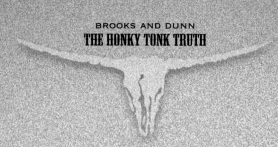
"For the most part we get along real good.
We aren't warm and fuzzy with each other.
We don't hug. We also don't come to blows."
— Kix

So, when three enchilada specials were just about gone, DuBois said, "Why don't you guys sit down and see if you can write a song."

"We just said, sure," Kix says. "What have we got to lose?"

Ronnie, who had mostly written songs by himself prior to moving to Nashville, was nervous about writing with someone else, especially a veteran like Kix who had been writing songs (including several #1's)

with different partners for years. Ronnie had only recently gotten his songwriting deal at Sony Tree and was a little put-off by the Nashville songwriting approach... *go to the office, partner-up, and write...every day.*

"Kix was probably thinking in the back of his mind, please don't make me baby-sit some new guy," Ronnie says.

Kix laughs and shakes his head, "I didn't feel like that at all."

"Ronnie's volatile and hot-headed and Kix ain't.
They learned to gee and haw, working mules, you know.
Give and take. I know they've had some discussions,
but I've never seen them in an argument."
—Danny Milliner

So Kix and Ronnie agreed to try to write together. If they hit it off, both said they would *consider* becoming a duo. DuBois says he thought the two would mesh for several reasons. They were around the same age (Ronnie 38, Kix 36), they were from the same region of the country (Texas, Louisiana), neither were new to the music business, both were productive songwriters, and DuBois says there was a similarity in the music they were making at the time. It got him to thinking.

DuBois had become acquainted with Kix's music courtesy of producer/ songwriter, Don Cook, who pitched a 5-song demo tape to Arista hoping to secure a solo deal for Kix. DuBois was more familiar with Ronnie's music. He had seen him perform in Oklahoma and had been given several demo tapes by engineer-turned-producer (and later, president of Virgin Records), Scott Hendricks, who met

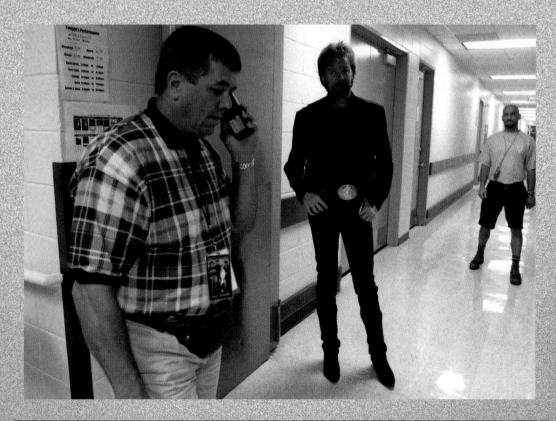

"Ronnie was always afraid that Kix would say something to upset someone," says bass player Danny Milliner.
"Like the first time they won Duo of the Year—we were playing in Omaha and Ronnie said, 'Don't get up there and talk about winning that award. These country people will turn on ya. They won't like you if you start bragging on yourself.'"
That night, Danny says, immediately after walking on stage, before even playing a note Kix yelled into his mike,
"Anybody see us on T.V. last night?"
"The crowd went completely nuts," Danny says.
Ronnie shook his head and fixed his eyes on his boots."

and worked with Ronnie after he won The Marlboro Talent Contest in 1988. DuBois had encouraged Ronnie to move to Nashville and even helped him land his songwriting deal.

At first, DuBois was considering separate deals for Kix and Ronnie. He admits the *Brooks & Dunn* duo idea wasn't an instant, cartoon light bulb over his head. In fact, he had already tried several combinations that did not work.

"Yeah," Hendricks says, "It was almost Brooks...and somebody else."

Months earlier, Hendricks and DuBois were on their way to see a University of Tennessee football game when DuBois brought up his duo idea.

"We were riding over in his truck," Hendricks says. "And Tim said, 'I'm gonna play you two guys. Tell me what you think.' And he played me Kix's stuff. I said, O.K. I get that. Then he played me another singer-songwriter in town, whose name I won't mention. He's a really good songwriter and singer, both. For some reason, though, I just did not hear that other guy working. He's really good, I just didn't hear that combination."

"It was Tim Mensy," Kix says. "Great singer. Great songwriter. He was trying to pursue a solo career." So Brooks and Mensy didn't work out, and instead, Hendricks says he reached into his bag and pulled out Ronnie Dunn's demo tape, which he had played for DuBois before.

"The first time I played it for him, months back, I said you've got to hear this voice," Hendricks says, "He said, 'Yeah, it's good, but I don't have a slot for it right now.' So, for the last year, I kept asking Tim, what about this Ronnie guy? That day, I put in the tape again. It had "Boot Scootin' Boogie," "Neon Moon," "She Used to Be Mine," and I think, "White Lightning." Three of those songs became number one songs. And this time, Tim goes, you're absolutely right. When he got back to town he introduced Kix and Ronnie."

So, after an $11 lunch, Kix and Ronnie got together, as so many Nashville musicians have for years, to try to write a couple of songs and possibly record them. Both had extremely low expectations.

"We were just kind of like, whatever," Ronnie says. "Let's try it and see what happens. That was really our attitude."

"I had the same attitude with Ronnie," Kix says. "It's like, hell, let's try to write some songs here and if we don't like each other, it's gonna be the end of it anyway. But I wasn't doing anything else, so..."

"We both did not have a lot of faith in the possibilities of our getting a record deal," Ronnie says. "Tim was very supportive about that happening. But after our first couple of meetings, I was not inspired, nor do I think Kix was. I didn't see a future there as writers, and certainly not as performers and partners."

Three weeks of relatively unproductive songwriting sessions followed. Then one day, Ronnie and Kix worked on a song Ronnie had started. He says that earlier that week, his wife, Janine, had given him one of those "newlywed, you better get it right this time, hoss" lectures. He says he left the room, grabbed his guitar and wrote the lines, *"I saw the light, I've been baptized by*

"During an awards show once," Ronnie says, "we were sharing a dressing room with Glen Campbell. I was nervous. There he was—Glen Campbell—bigger than life! We got to talk about songs. He said, 'I like all your songs except that one thing . . . that Boot . . . Whatever Scoot. Can you imagine singing that in your 40s?' "

the fire in your touch and the flame in your eyes…" Then he jotted down a title, "I'm a Changed Man."

Ronnie played the lines for Kix.

"I said, 'That's cool. I love the feel of it and everything,'" Kix says, "But 'I'm a *Brand New* Man' would meter a little better. And he goes, I like that. That's cool. So we kicked it around, started writing the verses and all that. Then we went over to [Don] Cook's house. We were working on something else and got stumped. Ronnie goes, 'You mind if I pull that thing out?' I said no. Cook heard it and right off the bat goes, 'I'm born to love again, I'm a brand new man!' We were like, 'Yeah! Do that!' It just hit him. That's what co-writing is about."

Soon after writing "Brand New Man," Kix and Ronnie wrote "My Next Broken Heart," again with Don Cook. They recorded those songs as demos with Cook and Hendricks co-producing. Combined with the demos they had already recorded separately, Ronnie and Kix had a strong package to deliver to Tim DuBois. One they both now believed in.

Arista loved it. Technically, *Brooks & Dunn* were now a duo. But both Ronnie and Kix, having had many separate disappointments in their solo careers, were taking things day by day.

"I don't think either one of us knew what was gonna happen or if this was something that we wanted to dedicate our lives to," Kix says. "Is this something where we're just gonna make a record and that'll be that? It wasn't like we were brothers. We're not a mother-daughter team. It's not a family thing. We didn't grow up in grade school together all our lives. So there was a lot of tiptoeing around and kind of trying to figure each other out."

While they were trying to figure each other out, they kept working on songs and began assembling a touring band. They weren't even really sure of how to categorize themselves. The only thing they knew is what they didn't want to be.

"There were a couple of guys a few years ago," Ronnie says. "Moe and Joe. They were kind of cheesy, real hard-core country. We didn't want to get into that kind of silly stuff. We wanted to have a little bit of legitimacy."

Ronnie remembers their first meeting with DuBois after he and Kix agreed to try the duo thing: "DuBois told us, 'Well, we want to make it like a real honky-tonk kind of thing.' We're all standing around going, What are they calling us…a honky-tonk band? Oh, *Hard Core Honky-Tonk*. O.K. We're a honky-tonk."

DuBois also told the guys there were three things they had to do to be successful. Ronnie and Kix allowed their minds to race during the pregnant pause that followed. Finally, DuBois told them: "Keep your boots on. Keep your jeans on. And keep it country."

Kix remembers saying, "We can do that."

So, Tim DuBois got his new hard-core honky-tonk duo a manager, Bob Titley, who represented Kathy Mattea. At first, Titley was reluctant to take on *Brooks & Dunn*. He says he hesitated because of the huge time commitment it takes to launch a new band and because he was fearful of managing a non-family duo.

"There had been no duo not related by blood that had survived more than a year or two in this business," Titley says. But Titley says he loved the music.

"I'm from Texas," he says. "Asleep at the Wheel is one of the first acts I worked with so I like honky-tonk music. I grew up

Ronnie's partner has become the proverbial *old, comfortable,(be-it-ever-so-energetic) shoe.*

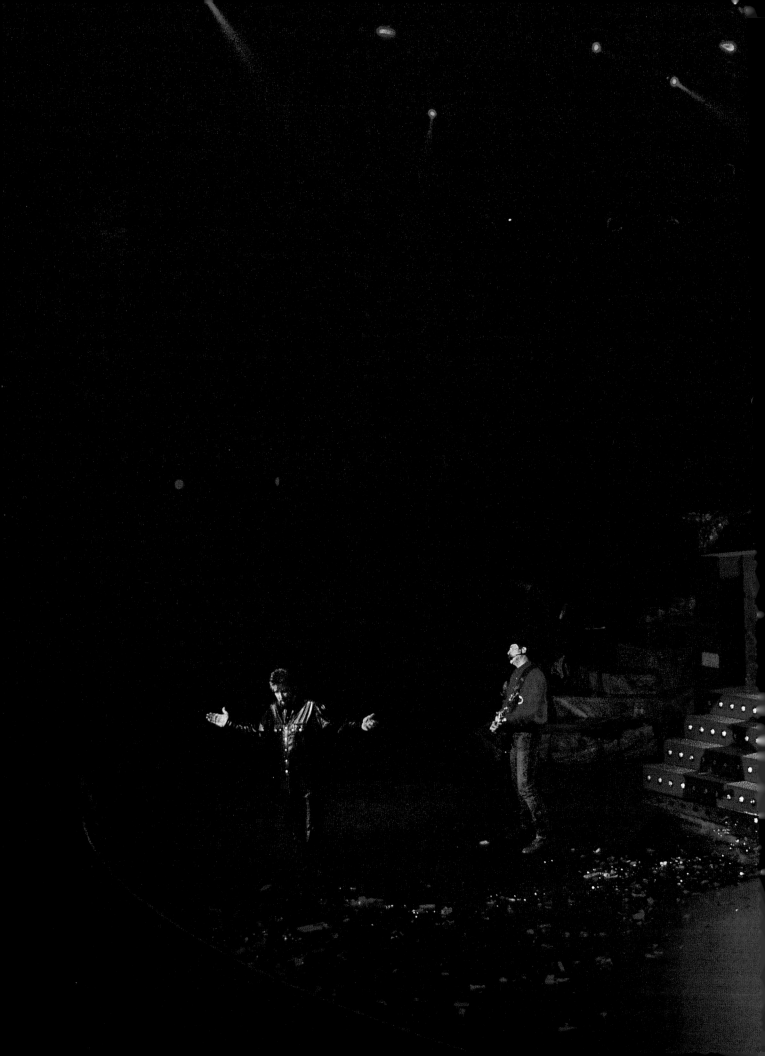

"We leave the profundity to Billy Ray Cyrus."
—Ronnie and Kix

in that world. I thought this would be a fun project. That it would sell gold in Texas."

As Titley saw it, his biggest task was to help keep them together. If they did that, he figured, they would have a few hits.

It was now time to get on stage. The first *Brooks & Dunn* showcase, for about 200 record company executives and select others, was played at The Ace of Clubs in Nashville in mid-April of 1991. The band played six songs. *B&D* bandleader, Danny Milliner, who played in several pre-*B&D* bands with Kix, says the night was a great success.

"People thought it rocked," Danny said. "It was loud and raucous and raw. They got the message. And Ronnie and Kix had a real chemistry together on stage."

Arista executives agreed.

"They thought we were wonderful," Kix says. "Luckily there was a girl with a fifth of Cuervo and a lot of shot glasses working the crowd before we came out."

Ronnie disagreed with the audience assessment of him and his new partner. In fact, he says he was mortified.

"I just thought we were awful," Ronnie says. "Terrible! I can never remember being so embarrassed playing in front of people. We took off

"Ronnie is actually a very outgoing human, but he hates for anybody to know it."

— Kix

on "Neon Moon" or something like that, and here goes Kix from this end of the stage to the next end. We hadn't played that long together and I thought Kix was so bizarre. I come from such a completely different performing background. I didn't have a clue what he was gonna do. He started jumping across the stage and doing this weird stuff. It freaked me out."

He says his wife, Janine, laughs when she remembers the shocked look on his face as he watched his new partner's stage antics. After the show, Ronnie talked to Danny Milliner about Kix's rowdy performance.

"I told Ronnie, you've got to get over that," Danny says, "Kix has always done this. I've been gored by a Telecaster more than once. I mean, just look at them big ol' feet!"

Ronnie didn't tell Kix how he felt right away.

"We never talk about that stuff," Ronnie says. "I just thought, hey, he's a grown man. Kix is real headstrong and we both have our separate egos. He doesn't talk about stuff about me, and I don't talk about stuff about him. We never have."

Ronnie also elected to keep his thoughts to himself because he didn't think they were going to be together that long anyway.

"I didn't think it was gonna work," he says. "I sincerely didn't. I just thought there's no way. We'll go to Texas and they'll kill us. Soon as this guy starts dancing across the stage, somebody's gonna take a shot."

But almost immediately, the partnership did work. It kept going. Records went to Number One. Tickets were selling.

"I was amazed that people would buy tickets to come see this fiasco," Ronnie says. "In all honesty. It amazes me! And Kix feels the same way. We couldn't believe it. Still can't."

After a couple of months, when it appeared this arranged marriage might not have to be annulled after all, Ronnie says he did talk to his partner about their contrasting performing styles. He told Kix, "Hey man, I come from this Okie thing where you stand up there and sing your song, and you might try settling down a little bit."

"I said, look," Kix says, "I been doing this thing a long time, too, man. But that microphone stand ain't an anchor, pal. You can take that mike and sing to that girl in the corner. Not just the people right in front of you."

A couple of months later, even though Ronnie still felt more comfortable singing into the microphone firmly planted in its stand, ("I wouldn't even hold it," he says), he had begun to appreciate Kix's style.

"Kix is a believer in doing anything you need to get the crowd going," Ronnie says. "A lot of times, I'd be up there singing a ballad or something and he'd be doing something — especially in the early days. Finally one day, I just said, 'Hey, if I'm in the middle of 'Neon Moon,' don't be bouncing across the stage on your head. Stick and hang there for three minutes. That's all you've got to do.'"

Kix remembers his response: "I'm like, man — you're standing out there like a stiff. Why don't you *do* something?"

Ronnie couldn't help it; he still had idealized pictures in his head.

"I came from the school that said you just stand there and deliver the song," he says. "I thought Emmylou Harris was just a goddess, that she could stand in one spot, flat-footed and just tear your heart out."

"Well, where I come from," Kix says, "we raise hell and jump out on tables and kick beer all over and all that stuff..."

Opposites attract? The yin and the yang? The agony and the ecstasy? Sonny and Cher? No one is quite sure. But two-hard-headed guys kept doing things their way and over a decade later, they're still together, collecting awards, piling up ticket sales, and racking up Top Ten hits. And they never argue...

"Right," Ronnie says. "We don't."

"Yes we do!" Kix says.

"Liar."

"You know we argue...why do you lie?"

"They're both savvy. They do a great job of making people feel at ease and important. A production assistant came up to me [once] and said, 'Hey, they know my name.' It goes a long way.
They're still as genuine as they were before they became famous."

— Mike Merriman, director of many B & D videos

Kix Brooks inside The Old Absinthe House,
his old Bourbon Street haunt.

THE ONE WITH THE HAT

KIX BROOKS leads a double life. On one side: Brooks & Dunn. Performing shows, writing and recording songs, tending to business decisions, attending award shows and charity functions. On the other side: the horse farm. Raising, breeding, riding and showing horses.

Kix , Barbara, and his two kids, Molly and Eric, live in an upscale development in suburban Brentwood, Tennessee. But eventually, Kix and Barb plan to live at the farm full-time where they plan to wear out their respective saddles.

"We're supposed to be selling horses, but Barb gets too attached to them," Kix says. "She's covered up in horses."

Every horse in the Brooks' stables has a story. Prieto is the horse Kix brought home after they co-starred together in the "My Maria" video. Angel, a paint mare, was Barb's first horse, a surprise gift from Kix in 1993.

Leon Eric Brooks, III, was born on May 12, 1955 in Shreveport, Louisiana. He was nicknamed "Kix" before he was born because he kicked non-stop in the womb. When Kix was four years old, his mother died of cancer. She was 32.

"I can remember it like it was yesterday," Kix says, "kissing her good-bye as the ambulance took her to the hospital."

Kix and his sister, Midge, were raised by his grandmother and his father, Leon Brooks, a straight-talking oil company engineer. His father later remarried and had two more kids, Lisa and Ben. Kix credits his father, who died in 1998, with giving him the push he needed to "make it".

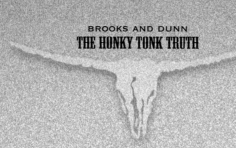

"He always encouraged me to be a big fish in a big pond," Kix says. "I remember when I was getting out of high school I was thinking of asking him to co-sign a note so I could buy a bar in Shreveport. I had a great local following there and I wanted to be the headliner. He was like, 'Get out of here. If you're serious about what you're doing, go for the big time. If you want to be in the music business, then be in the music business.'"

Kix says he always had a lot of respect for his dad's "brain power," even though he had no interest in becoming an engineer like his father.

"It made me feel good that someone I respected as much as him gave me credit that my ambitions weren't frivolous," Kix says. "He had the attitude, do whatever you want. But take it seriously."

When *Brooks & Dunn* won Entertainer of the Year at The ACM awards in 1996, Kix says it was one of the greatest moments of his life for all the obvious reasons.

"But having my dad there," Kix says, "that was really incredible to have him see that."

Kix's hometown of Shreveport was also the home of KWKH and *The Louisiana Hayride*, a Grand Ol' Opry-type radio show. This country music claim-to-fame, combined with other musical goings-on (Cajun, jazz, blues, bluegrass), certainly influenced the young, musically-inclined Kix, who learned to play the ukulele at age six.

Soon after, he learned to play the guitar by listening to Hank Williams and Johnny Horton songs. Next, he formed a band and again there was a Williams-Horton connection: the mother of one of his classmate's was Billy Jean Horton, Johnny Horton's widow. Billy Jean had also once been married to Hank! Kix remembers seeing Horton's gold records on the wall of their home where he played his first paying gig at his classmate's 12th birthday party. But he was more excited about the payday.

"We got a buck a piece," Kix laughs. "Five big ones. I remember looking at the five and popping it."

Country music was in Shreveport's soul. A musician couldn't escape it. Kix says he indeed listened to KWKH, but during the frequent airings of the Gospel Hour, he switched to the pop station. Then, finding the pop tunes "too teeny bopper" he switched to jazz and the blues music.

"I always listened to Diana Ross, Otis Redding, Sam Cooke," Kix says. "That music had so much soul it just seemed so much better to me than all that other crap — the teeny bopper stuff. Then, when I was 13, the rock stuff started influencing me too. My first bands were schizophrenic. We played everything from 'Hey Good Lookin' to 'Gloria'."

Kix came home from the *My Maria* shoot with more than just dust in his boots.
His souvenir from this trip? Prieto, the gorgeous horse he clung to in all those "rearing back" shots.

"Kix is fearless," Ronnie says.
"He has absolutely no inhibitions whatsoever. I mean, that's a grown man with children."

"When you are driving a race car, everything is out of your mind except the next turn. Race car driving takes your mind away from everything or else you are hitting the wall," explains Kix.

"Kix is real level-headed when it comes to business decisions and stuff like that. He's real calm and pretty much on an even keel. You wouldn't think that by seeing him live, but he's really laid back. We're probably just the opposite of how we seem on stage."

— Ronnie

Kix attended boarding school at Sewanee Military Academy for four years. After graduating, he enrolled briefly at Southern Methodist University, intending to study classical guitar technique. He soon transferred to Louisiana Tech where he majored in theater arts and speech. During this time, Kix says, Jerry Jeff Walker, Waylon Jennings and Willie Nelson were really stirring things up.

"Their music had a huge influence on me," he says. "That's when I really started sharpening the pencil up. The songs I wrote were terrible, but I was really inspired. And I really wanted to do it."

Then, in 1975, he decided to take a break from college.

"I told my dad, I think I'll take a little break and just kinda hang out for a while," Kix says. "My dad said, 'Oh, you think so?'"

Leon, who was a contractor for the Alaska Pipeline, quickly arranged for Kix to work during his "break" — in Fairbanks, Alaska. Heading to the tundra appealed to Kix's adventurous spirit. Soon, he began playing in local clubs.

"We started in Fairbanks and went up north of the Yukon," Kix says. "It was damn cold. Between 30 and 60 below. Dark all the time. In the winter it was brutal — nothing but snow and ice."

Ronnie Dunn says the experience of working with tough, rough-and-tumble co-workers never left Kix.

"He carries it with him today," Ronnie says. "He talks about it all the time. Not bragging, but talking about how ruthless it was. I know, because my dad was in the pipeline business too. They've got a certain macho approach to things. If you hit your hand with a hammer, you just say, 'Well, yeah. It hurts. But, c'mon. We've got pipe to load.' That attitude helps a lot of times, because I'll get bummed out real quick. My feelings are way out front and I'll read a review or something I don't like and just go off. I call it my 'Okie factor.' I'm ready to quit the whole business, throw in the towel and go home. But Kix just goes, 'Hey, man, that's just part of it. Just roll with it. Go!'"

Kix says he was thinking about his fellow-pipeliners during one of the best moments of his life. Early in the partnership of *Brooks & Dunn*, they played a festival that also featured Merle Haggard, a huge hero to both Ronnie and Kix.

Kix sent their road manager to ask Haggard to autograph his guitar. When he returned, Kix grabbed the guitar, "Did you get it?" His face dropped when he saw there was no autograph. The road manager told Kix that Merle said he would sign it, but Kix had to come get it himself.

Kix asked Ronnie to come with him. (Answer: "No way, hoss.") Kix took a deep breath, tucked his guitar under his arm and went to meet Merle.

"I remember stepping on his bus and it was like walking that corridor to Oz," Kix says. "He was just fixing to go on stage. But he said, 'Sit down!' And he took my guitar and played it before he signed it. His road manager's going, 'Hag...you're supposed to be on!' And he's going, 'Hang on a second.' And I kept thinking, what would those guys think now if they could see me sitting here talking to Merle Haggard like he knows me! To all those truck drivers that I was around pipelining, *Haggard* was a sacred word."

After Kix left Alaska, he returned to Louisiana Tech and graduated. Soon after, he went north again, this time to Maine, where he worked doing TV/radio production and writing copy and jingles for his sister's advertising agency. At night, he played in local coffee houses. Then one night, he went to a party where he met a striking brunette named Barbara who owned a fabric store in town. Even though he had been dating the party's hostess, he asked for Barbara's number.

"She was the better deal," Kix says.

Barb says she felt no guilt since the hostess had confided in her that she was in love with another man.

Even though he'd found his girl, Kix found life in Maine a little sedate. He soon took off for New Orleans to fulfill a

"You can go in Kix's bus and see that he's just kicked back," says NASCAR star and pal Dale Earnhardt. "It's not like he's in there, *Oh! I gotta practice! I gotta go!* He's just like, whatever. Nothing ever rattles him. Ronnie on the other hand has a group of people around him. The family's around. Ha! Ha! Ronnie comes over to Kix's bus to hang out! To get some quiet time!"

*"Kix dresses bad now," Ronnie says.
"But he's come a long way."*

lifelong dream of being part of the Big Easy music scene. He wanted to live the life he heard about in Tom Waits' songs. On Bourbon Street, musicians played all night, every night, to rowdy crowds that were close enough to touch. Kix says all his solo performances during college primed him well.

"I played hog killings standing on picnic tables and stuff like that," he says. "So I knew how to attract attention and make a lot of noise. I had to be obnoxious for a couple of hours to survive."

Kix says he had to be inventive to deal with the boisterous crowds.

"One night," he says, "the doors [that opened onto the street] were just full. They were all screaming at me. So, I got this blank pistol and just popped the cap off it. They were all looking for bullet holes! It worked pretty good for a couple of days, then the cops came in and said man, you gotta quit doing that."

Kix got into a groove and played Bourbon Street bars night after night, most of them without the benefit of his cap gun. He played for cash. Fifty bucks a night.

"I didn't pay taxes," Kix says. "I didn't have car insurance. My rent wasn't but $150 a month. So I was living like a Sultan."

Performers in the French Quarter had an all-night world all their own.

"I'd play from nine o'clock till midnight, or sometimes three," Kix says, "Then I'd go down to The Blues Room and listen to Luther Kent play. After that, a whole group of strippers and people who worked in the The Quarter would go to this warehouse place where we'd just drink, shoot pool, and chill out till daylight. It was a big hang. There'd be five or six poker games going on. People talking, sitting on bean bag chairs. I'd go home after sunrise."

Ultimately, there were a few glitches in Kix's nightlife career. One of his gigs — playing an upscale bar with shiny railings and hanging plants — didn't work out at all.

"The owner was really nice, giving me a chance," he says. "But one day he says, 'I don't think you're quite right for this place.' I guess I wasn't the fern-bar type. Plus he wanted me to play cover songs, like John Denver, and that wasn't my thing."

Kix was more into guys like Roy Head and George Thorogood "who would jump on your table and kick beer all over you." Besides his own stuff, he liked to sing songs from the 30s and 40s, like "Ain't Misbehavin'" and "Nobody Loves You When You're Down and Out." He had a great time playing this music. But once again, he was restless.

Jody Williams, Kix's Sewanee Academy roommate, was working in writer/publisher relations at Broadcast Music, Inc. (BMI), one of two agencies that collect and distribute money to songwriters and publishers for the public performance (mostly radio airplay) of their songs.

Jody had long been encouraging Kix to come to Nashville. But Kix was determined to try New Orleans first. After many months and countless late nights, Kix got the push he needed however. His landlady found out he was illegally sharing his apartment and kicked him out. He figured it was Nashville time.

"Yeah," Kix says. "It was like when I quit playing banjo. At this cocktail party, this lady came up to me and said, 'My husband's always wanted to play banjo. How much do they cost?' I said, 'Like this one?' and sold her my banjo! It was the last time I ever touched one! Going to Nashville was the same kind of thing."

In 1980, 25-year-old banjo-less Kix Brooks drove from New Orleans to Nashville in a shell of a van with a beat-up lounge chair serving as his passenger seat.

He immediately found a one-room efficiency and began peeling through the wad of 100 dollar bills he'd saved from New Orleans. The money went fast. Kix worked a series of odd jobs: at a convenience store, in a warehouse, as a temporary day laborer, and as a security guard for rock and roll shows making $30 a night.

But music was on his mind. He began writing and showing up for open mike or "writer's nights" familiar to every aspiring Nashville musician.

"I was writing songs I thought were good and hanging out on Music Row, beating on doors," Kix says. "I knew enough people to play songs for major publishers and they'd listen. But after that, they'd always be out to lunch when I called."

But Kix kept at it. Barbara moved to Nashville and they got married on August 1, 1981. He was digging in. Along the way he caught several encouraging breaks.

The first came when Bob Doyle, who later managed Garth Brooks, saw him perform at a writer's night and hooked him up with Don Gant's Golden Bridge Music, where Kix became a staff songwriter earning a draw against future royalties of his songs.

His first big success came when The Oak Ridge Boys included his tune, "Old Kentucky Song," on their album, *Bobbie Sue*.

Kix later signed on as a staff writer at Tree Publishing (now Sony ATV Tree). Throughout the 80s, Kix was incredibly productive. Several of the songs he wrote or co-wrote became big hits for other artists, including "Modern Day Romance"

You can leave your hat on.

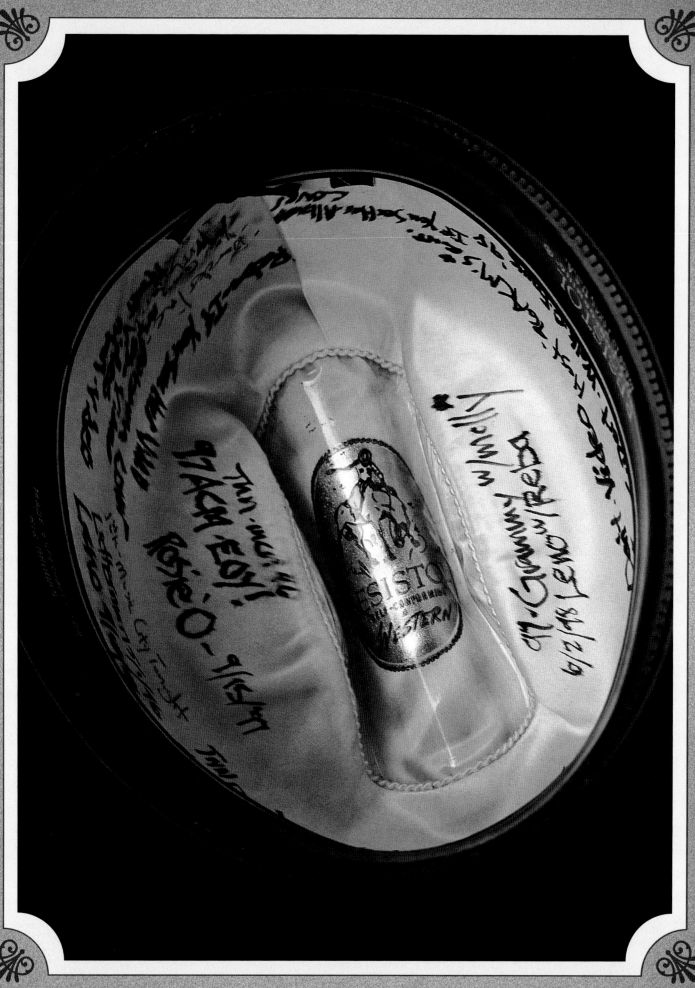

"I think I kept my eyes shut for the first 15 years I sang."
— *Ronnie Dunn*

THE TALL ONE WITH THE BEARD

RONNIE GENE DUNN was born on June 1, 1953 in Coleman, Texas, the first child of Gladys and Jesse Eugene Dunn. Two sisters, Denise and Renee, and a brother, Johnny, followed.

Ronnie's childhood was spent on the move, from Texas to South Central Arkansas, to Tulsa, Oklahoma, back to Texas... He lived in 33 different towns before he turned 18. Ronnie's father, Jesse, worked mostly for an oil pipeline company. Several times, he was transferred. But according to Ronnie, it was usually his father's drinking that led to the moves.

"He didn't seem to be able to hold down a job," Ronnie says.

At home, Ronnie and his siblings endured the constant clash of their rowdy, hard-drinking father and their mild-mannered, Baptist mother.

"My mother was so diehard straight," Ronnie says. "She was against any kind of drinking."

The up-side to life in the Dunn house was music. Jesse was a talented singer and guitar player. His preference: hard-core, traditional country tunes.

"He was real dynamic," Ronnie says. "A real character. He was a lot of fun. He just lived music. He worked in the oil fields and stuff like that, but the radio was always on. He'd come home and pick up his guitar. His friends would come over and play and sing all night long."

But with the playing and singing came beer drinking.

"I was always enthralled with Dwight Yoakam, who has such style and a great visual image. If truth be known, I just want to be Dwight Yoakam."

– Ronnie

"And my mom wouldn't go for that," Ronnie says, "so it would always end on a real down note."

Jesse had his musical "15 minutes of fame" as lead singer/guitar player for The Fox Four Five, the house band at KRBC, a radio station in Abilene, Texas, that broadcast a concert series every Saturday night. The band also cut a couple of records for a small label.

Ronnie says, "I can remember as a kid, once or twice he took us on vacation and we went through Nashville. I don't know if he'd tried to take his tapes to somebody, that kind of deal. He'd tried for the longest time to break in. That's more what he wanted to do. Everything else he did in life was just to support his family. Music. That was his dream."

Ronnie says there were always guitars around the house, one in particular: a top-of-the-line Martin acoustic that was his dad's favorite. This guitar was so valuable to Jesse that he actually drove across town during a tornado to remove it from the house and put it in a safe place.

One night his father had a jam session with his friends. He came home drunk and Ronnie's parents began to argue. Ronnie, who was 12 years old, heard a scream and a crash in the bedroom. He walked in and was horrified to see that his father had opened the Martin guitar case in front of Ronnie's mother and stomped the guitar to bits.

Ronnie says he doesn't remember his father playing much after that. But when Ronnie turned 14, Jesse bought him his own bass guitar.

"I think it cost $250, which was a ton of money," Ronnie says. "He taught me to play it by ear."

Ronnie was a quick study where music was concerned.

"In school, English, math, I couldn't care less about them!" Ronnie says. "But in music I made straight A's no matter what. It always came natural. It was always something that was just there."

Also "just there" for young Ronnie Dunn: an incredible singing voice. But he was terribly shy, so it took a lot of prodding from his father ("Sing! Go!") before Ronnie would even try.

"I'd go in my room and not come out," Ronnie says. "It was just like learning to swim. He'd throw you in the water and say, 'Here you go, sink or swim.' It taught me a lot about singing. I think I kept my eyes shut for the first fifteen years I sang."

In high school, Ronnie played bass guitar and sax. After graduation, he enrolled at Hardin-Simmons University in Abilene, Texas, to study psychology and theology. His paternal grandmother, who had always encouraged him, agreed to pay his tuition. His intention was to become a Baptist minister.

"I was torn between this side of the family over here — the staunch religious side of the family, the Baptists," Ronnie says. "Then I had my dad over here — the complete epitome of the all-American hell-raiser. I had both influences there all the time. I was gonna go figure it out for myself. I tried the complete religious side for a while."

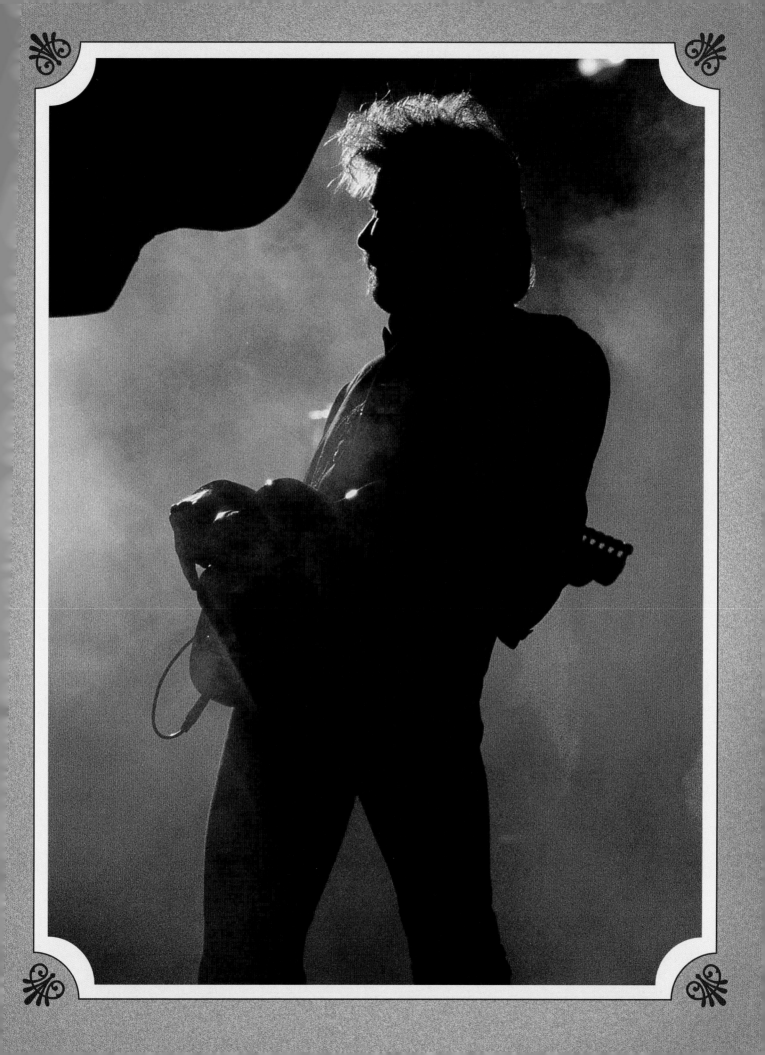

*"I get bad blood sugar," Ronnie says.
"Usually the crew guys keep a sandwich
taped to an amp for me."*

Ronnie and Haley Dunn

Soon, he transferred to Abilene Christian College. During his second year, he realized it was unlikely he would ever become a preacher.

"For two years I worked on it until I realized that part of being a preacher was having to stand up in front of people and talk," Ronnie says. "I knew I couldn't speak in public."

Despite his shyness, Ronnie got up on stage every weekend and played bass guitar in pick-up bands. He had no problem staying busy.

"I was on a call list because I could play by ear well," Ronnie says. "I could wing-it without knowing the songs. Plus, I had my own amp."

Every weekend, he'd take his amp with its two, big, 15-inch cabinets, and stuff it in the back seat of his tiny, run-down brown Mercury Capri and drive it 100 miles to the VFW in Stanford, Texas. Or to an abandoned armory in Waco. Or Midland...

"The only way to drive," Ronnie says, "was to push the seats up front as far as they'd go. I had to drive hunched forward over the steering wheel."

Playing bass, essentially in the background, suited Ronnie's shy personality. Then one night, he got pulled up front to sing lead on one song. When his bandmates heard his voice, it was pretty much decided. Shy or not: this boy was staying up-front.

During his college years, Ronnie experienced a textbook Freudian tug. By day, he was fulfilling his mother's dream: studying religion. By night, he was living his father's dream: playing in honky-tonks. Eventually, the two lifestyles collided.

"I was playing in bars," Ronnie says. "And they [ACC administrators] didn't like that. I got called into the dean's office one day. He said, 'You know our policy at the university is you can't frequent these places. You're going to have to make a choice.' I was pretty disillusioned at the time — I wasn't the best student in the world. So I decided to try the music for a while."

Ronnie began playing in any Texas beer joint that would take him. It wasn't long, though, until he fixed his sights on Tulsa, where his parents had recently moved. He decided to join them there after his mother sent him a newspaper clipping about Tulsa-based Jim Halsey, who Ronnie says was the biggest agent in country music at the time.

"I think [my parents] were thinking that I'd go there and work for a while, see what the real world is like, and high-tail it back to college."

But that didn't happen. Instead, Ronnie got busy with music. He also got a "day job" selling clothes in a rock-and-roll store. (Although it was the disco era, Ronnie swears he did not use his employee discount to partake of the platform shoes.)

"I thought, man this is it!" Ronnie says. "What a great way to make contacts. I met people in Eric Clapton's band. That's how I got to know them."

He ended up playing gigs with some of his customers, and soon formed his own band, known simply as *Ronnie Dunn*. Soon, Ronnie was headlining at Duke's Country, a huge country dance club, playing songs by Merle Haggard, John Prine, The Allman Brothers, and old classics including "You Don't Know Me." He'd also slip in some of his originals. The band, somewhat reluctantly, played Top 40 songs too. As dance club headliners, they had to be ready to play requests at a moment's notice.

"It was degrading," Ronnie says. "You show up and you're a human jukebox."

Then *Ronnie Dunn* became the house band at another huge dance club, Tulsa City Limits. (At one point, the bass player in this band was Garth Brooks' sister, Betsy.)

At Tulsa City Limits in the early 80s, the *Urban Cowboy*-inspired patrons wanted to dance, and club owners wanted them to dance. But Ronnie wanted to play his own songs. So he wrote a song about the whole "Friday night, running from club-to-club lifestyle" and called the song "Boot Scootin' Boogie." He meant it to have deeper meaning, but mostly, it got Tulsa club-goers out of their chairs and into dance lines.

One exciting aspect of playing the big clubs, Ronnie says, was opening for some of his favorite performers.

"I opened for everybody you could imagine," Ronnie says. "George Jones, Rodney Crowell, Rosanne Cash."

Those were the good nights. But good as they were, the money wasn't great. So Ronnie's band also booked other gigs wherever they could get them.

Question from the Q&A session at the Brooks & Dunn Fan Club party (Fan Fair 1988):
"Boxers of briefs?"
"You think anybody's wearing boxers under those pants?"

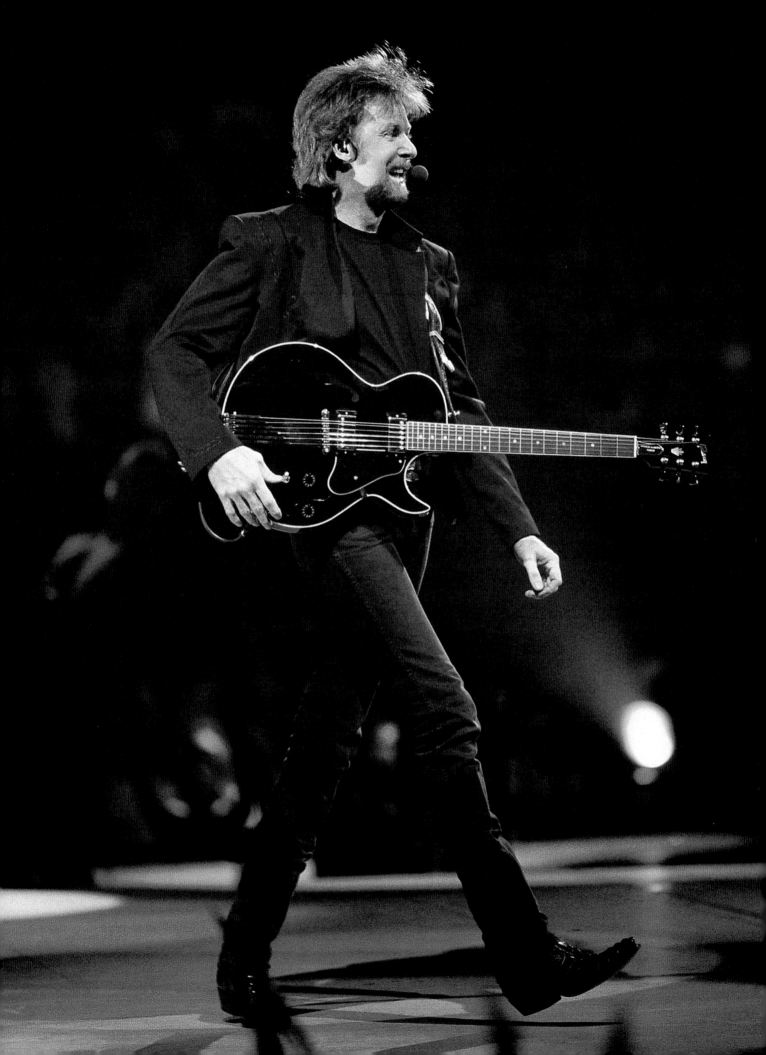

*"We were in the studio recording 'Mama Don't Get Dressed Up for Nothing.'
We had it really rocking. Ronnie was yelling, 'Yeah! It's like the Stones! C'mon!
Do it like Keith Richards!' Then somebody says, 'Hey, Merle Haggard's coming in.'
Ronnie's whole demeanor changed. He was like a kid caught blasting the stereo in the house
and dad is standing in the doorway. He's like, 'Turn it down. Merle's here.'
So we tried playing it, you know, toned down, then we just quit for a while.
Merle stayed around for a while, told some stories. Then, after he left, we turned it back up.
But do you blame him? Ronnie's a big Merle Haggard fan.
Merle is real anti-contemporary, very true to the old styles.
We didn't want to be responsible for ruining country music!"*

—guitar player Brent Mason

They played one club that looked like a chicken house, and a rock and roll club where the patrons stood and silently stared as Ronnie sang Rodney Crowell and Bellamy Brothers songs. Then there was the Cherokee Nation Hoedown where Ronnie stood in front of bales of hay after the show to sign autographs. Ronnie also played countless nights in dark, rough-and-tumble beer joints, such as The Beeline Lounge in Tulsa. He always made it a point to enter and leave through the back door.

"One time, there were two brothers," Ronnie says. "One killed another one out in the parking lot while we were there. He dragged his body out on the highway to disguise that it had been hit with a tire tool! There was a big fight. The stage was way down here on this end and there were some pool tables in the back. We never stopped playing. That's the biggest rule when a fight breaks out. Keep playing. Never stop."

Ronnie at home in Nashville, Tennessee.

Besides paying his dues playing live, Ronnie began breaking into recording. He made several demos with Leon Russell's Shelter Records. One night he brought home one of the demos and played it for his father. His dad had been drinking and he criticized the song, telling Ronnie "it wasn't country enough."

"All the anxiety I had against him for years came out at that point," Ronnie says. "I remember him standing up and acting like he was going to hit me. We got into a hot discussion. I finally told him to kiss my butt. It was the first time I ever stood up to him. I told him that's the end of that, pal, and he stood up. I never missed eye contact with him. Then I flat laid him out. I remember the look in his eyes falling backwards. It was the culmination of years of that stuff, fighting with my mother, verbal abuse, years of frustration, and it all came out then. We didn't talk for two years."

It seemed that the confrontation made Ronnie more determined to succeed. He got a big break when Jim Halsey (the agent featured in the clipping his mother sent him) asked him to be the first artist on his new label, Churchill Records. Ronnie recorded several songs, including two, "It's Written All Over Your Face" and "She Put the Sad in His Songs," that hit the national charts in 1983 and 1984.

But Churchill Records had distribution problems and soon folded. By the mid-80s, work in the clubs had slowed. Ronnie got a job in a liquor store to support his first

wife and their two young children, Whitney (born on December 22, 1980) and Jesse (born on July 12, 1983).

The stress during this time took its toll. Ronnie and his wife divorced. But happily, he and his father reconciled.

"We slowly got back into the loop," Ronnie says. "Thank God, he straightened up. He joined the church and went completely the other way. He stayed that way until he died."

Ronnie continued writing songs and playing the clubs whenever he could. Then one day, his drummer and manager, Jamie Oldaker (who had toured with Eric Clapton for 11 years), spotted "one of those cardboard standup things" in a convenience store, filled out a form, and entered Ronnie in The 1988 Marlboro Country Music National Talent Roundup. He didn't tell Ronnie about it until later.

"I laughed at him and said, 'Nobody ever wins those things,'" Ronnie says. "I thought it was so corny — I was way too cool to be in a music contest."

Regardless, just before the deadline, Ronnie sent in a tape of three songs, including two covers: "Holed Up in Some Honky Tonk" and "You Don't Know Me," plus his own song, "Boot Scootin' Boogie." Ronnie was accepted for the first round.

Over 3,800 contestants competed in 19 cities in the first round. Ronnie's band won their city. As Tulsa's Local Winner, they took home $7500 and an invitation to open Tulsa's Marlboro Tour show.

Charlie Crow, Tony King, Ronnie Dunn, and Jimmy Stewart during Spiritual Week performance at Franklin Academy, 1998

Next came the semifinals at The Stockyard Restaurant's Bullpen Lounge in Nashville. The Grand Prize: $30,000 and a recording session with successful Nashville producer Barry Beckett and engineer Scott Hendricks. Ronnie won.

The money was desperately needed, and the recording session would change Ronnie's life. But initially, performing on the Marlboro Tour was the most thrilling aspect of winning the Grand Prize. Ronnie opened for Ricky Skaggs, Kathy Mattea, Randy Travis, Alabama, Restless Heart, Southern Pacific, and Highway 101. At the final show in Tulsa, Ronnie opened for his hero, Merle Haggard.

After the tour, Ronnie returned to Tulsa to plot his next move. The $30,000 prize, which was split six ways, didn't last long. The demos he had recorded in Nashville were making the rounds. Then Tim DuBois, a well-respected producer who was starting a new record label (Arista Nashville), came to see Ronnie in Oklahoma. DuBois told Ronnie if he moved to Nashville, he would get a record deal. But Ronnie had been disappointed before, and his kids were in Oklahoma. He was torn.

Meanwhile, Ronnie had begun dating Janine Patch, the young widow of a coal magnate whom he met when his band performed at one of her parties. Janine was passionate about Ronnie's talent and pushed him to move to Nashville. At first,

they made trips back and forth between Tulsa and Nashville, putting over 100,000 miles on their car the first year. But the long commute wasn't working, personally or professionally.

Janine and Ronnie were married in her Welch, Oklahoma, mansion, just before it was sold at auction. Janine had lost the coal mining business and was forced to sell everything to pay off debts. The newlyweds literally had nothing more to lose.

"I was working this job," Ronnie says, "driving a tractor mowing 600 acres. There was no one around but me. I stopped the tractor. I walked out to this field all by myself, and I got on my knees. I was thinking about faith and how I just couldn't make it happen. I'd made all the right moves and done everything humanly possible, and it was still not happening. So, all by myself... on my knees... for the first time in my life it clicked and I realized in order to accomplish things through faith you really have to put actions behind them. You can't expect a house to be built right in front of you. You've got to go get it."

So Ronnie got back on the tractor, went in the house, and boldly called Arista president Tim DuBois. Tim told Ronnie it must be "karma," because he was just looking for his number. He wanted to ask if *Asleep at the Wheel* could record "Boot Scootin' Boogie." (Ronnie said yes.) Tim also mentioned the record deal again.

"I was always screwing up lyrics,"
Ronnie says.

Ronnie and Janine moved to Nashville, and Janine's good friends, none other than June Carter and Johnny Cash, invited the Dunns to live in a log home on their property in Hendersonville, Tennessee. ("Just 'til Ronnie gets dug in," June said.) The Cashes would drop by occasionally, bringing a small gift or a piece of furniture. Johnny even gave Ronnie one of his suits.

"Here comes this black Mercedes in front of the house," Ronnie says. "Tires squealing, all this stuff. Here he comes, a big rock-and-roll stop in front of the house. And he gets out of the car — you know how reckless he is — and big! He pulls this suit out, hands it to me and says, 'Here. Got ya a suit. Don't let June hear about it. She'll kill me!' She knows how valuable those suits are!"

A few darts later, and after changing the bell bottoms to boot-cut legs, Ronnie wore the suit during the photo shoot for *Brand New Man*.

Soon after arriving in Nashville, Ronnie secured a writing contract with Sony Tree Publishing. He received a $250 per week salary, which was a draw against future song royalties. There was another songwriter at Sony Tree who Ronnie met not much later. His name was Kix Brooks.

On thier first tour, Ronnie, who felt more comfortable singing into a microphone firmly planted in its stand, began holding the mike. "I didn't want people in the front row to see that I was shaking."

ROAD DOGS

In 1991, Brooks & Dunn hit the road. As a brand new band (their first record wasn't even released yet), they were booked mostly into small clubs or in bigger venues as the opening act for better-known artists. Their first show was in Muskogee, Oklahoma, opening for Steve Wariner and Moe Bandy. They played for less than 30 minutes.

A blur of other shows followed. Fan Fair in Nashville. Billy Bob's in Texas. Then came several stops on the Marlboro Tour, opening for The Marshall Tucker Band and .38 Special, among others.

Band leader Danny Milliner was there the first time B&D played Kansas City, which had just been blanketed with a snow storm. "There were about 200 people," Danny says. "The glamour was killing us."

Danny remembers another even smaller crowd at Austin's AquaFest. "We played at 5:30 in the afternoon with the sun in our eyes to 13 people. Then a year later, we closed the same show with about 25,000 people!"

When B&D's first single, "Brand New Man," went to Number One, life on the road began to change. The crowds in the clubs swelled to standing room only. Kix and Ronnie saw fans in the crowd mouthing the words to their song. Then, when Brooks & Dunn were only six months into their first club tour, they were invited to open for Reba McEntire. In the fall of 1991, they played their first arena gigs as Reba's opening act. Ronnie says at first, they were scared to death.

"It was the first time we played where the lights weren't burning the top of my head," Ronnie said.

Brooks & Dunn quickly got comfortable in front of big crowds, which was a plus, since they soon would be headlining themselves. (Later, in 1997 and 1998, B&D actually co-headlined with Reba on two separate tours.)

TV host Ralph Emory, while interviewing Kix and Ronnie for his *On the Record* program, told them he went skiing with Reba in 1991 and she wore her Brooks & Dunn cap on the slopes every day.

"We worked for free if she would wear that hat skiing..."

Kix has roots in New Orleans and he saw B&D's first visit to The Big Easy as headliners in 1992 as a chance for a royal homecoming. He led Ronnie and the gang on a bar crawl of the French Quarter. Kix and company dropped into old haunts, such as The Old Absinthe House on Bourbon Street.

Making their way through the streets, Kix stopped abruptly in front of a karaoke bar and peered in the window. It was lively and packed with people.

"Don't even think about it!" Ronnie said.

Kix asked then-tour manager Eric Shinault to go in and see if they had any Brooks & Dunn songs on their karaoke machine. "Check the juke box, too! We don't need the words! Or, maybe we do."

Eric returned triumphant. The bar had "Brand New Man" on its machine.

"C'mon, Dunn!" Kix said, grabbing his partner by the elbow.

Kix dragged Ronnie to the stage. Ronnie was laughing so hard he was doubled over on his stool. Somehow, between hoots and heckling from their entourage, they managed to make it through the song. As they walked off the stage, they heard a woman say to her friends, "Well, they sure look like 'em but they can't sing a lick!"

Getting the whole Brooks & Dunn circus from town to town is a huge production. There are trucks full of equipment and sets, and several buses follow behind carrying crew and band members.

Today, Ronnie and Kix each have their own tour bus. The band (9 guys and the tour manager) also share a bus. B&D buses are luxurious by road musician's standards: there's air-conditioning, a refrigerator, shower, bathroom, and satellite TV. (The next time the B&D buses pull into an arena, take note. If the driver makes an excessive amount of 3-point turns, he's trying to get a better position for the satellite.)

But in the early days, things were a bit more rustic.

B&D's first tour bus (which carried the road manager, merchandise manager, and the whole band) was a Model 10 Eagle, which is much smaller than today's buses. It featured two lounges (one in front and one in back), a small bathroom, and curtained sleeping bunks in the middle.

"When Kix goes on stage, it's literally like a drug to him, I swear! It's almost frightening. He gets a glaze over his eyes, I mean it's absolutely psychotic! He tears up guitars all the time. That's just how he is."

-Ronnie

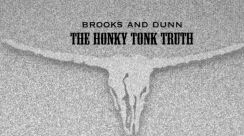

"I've been in the emergency room a bunch of times...
I'm real clumsy but I've got a lot of confidence so I fall down all the time."

— Kix

For weeks at a time, ten grown men spent night after night together on this bus, mostly in the front lounge because the back was piled with B&D T-shirts and merchandise.

"The one thing that sticks out in my mind the most about that period is when we lost the T-shirt guy in Bakersfield," Kix recalls. "He was with us on the bus. It was one of our first big nights selling T-shirts in L.A. — a thousand bucks worth, which for us then was a big night. We were all real tight-knit. We partied real hard. Then he didn't make bus call the next day. And the last somebody had seen him he was getting in a car with a bunch of tattooed guys at three in the morning. We were all sitting around the next day. It was like, we've got to go to Bakersfield and do a show and one of our troops didn't make it back. It really freaked us out. We were really afraid that he was dead, but he just went on a binge and spent all the money. By the time he called two days later, he had $10 left. Wanted to know if we could help him."

Kix took up rollerblading and in 1995, he started bringing his skates on the road. "It was a great way to throw the bus off ya," he said. Kix often slapped on a baseball hat and went skating in or around arenas where B&D's crew were setting up for the night's show. Kix decided it would be more fun if he had skating companions, so he offered to buy the band skates. Three guys took him up on his offer: Jimmy Stewart, Troy Klontz, and Dwain Rowe.

One day the blading band traveled nearly 20 miles along the Colorado River.

Dwain, who had just slicked on sunscreen, took an unfortunate tumble down a huge hill. "The grass was all stuck to him," Jimmy says. "He looked like the scarecrow in the *Wizard of Oz*!" If that weren't humbling enough, the guys, worried about being late for sound check, had to call a cab to take them back.

"Haven't missed a show yet," Troy smiles.

As any road musician will tell you, there are certain "bus rules" that must be adhered to for a group of grown men to get along in a very small space. One such rule on the Brooks & Dunn band bus—in the restroom, *peeing only*. Anything else shall be done before or after a trip, or during planned pit stops.

One afternoon in 1996, the band was traveling through the Midwest. The bus was just 30 miles from its destination when rookie fiddle player Jimmy Stewart announced he had to stop. It was an absolute emergency, Jimmy said. The driver reluctantly agreed. He pulled into a Steak n' Shake and told Jimmy he'd better hurry. No one else was permitted to get out. The driver wanted to be back on the highway immediately.

After more than 10 minutes, his bandmates became suspicious.

"He better not be getting something to eat," grumbled tour manager Scott Edwards.

Then, Jimmy came bounding up the bus stairs carrying a bag of onion rings. The next day, Jimmy stood trial in "crew court." His sentence: to wear an onion necklace for an entire day.

Jo Dee Messina was touring with *B&D* as one of their opening acts in 1996. She was well aware of Ronnie, Kix and crew's reputation for road gags and had become so paranoid waiting for them to strike that she decided to beat them to it. The tour landed in Largo, Maryland, just outside of Washington, D.C., early one November day for a show that evening. When Kix and Ronnie headed into the arena for a sound-check, Jo Dee took the opportunity to cram both their buses full of helium balloons.

Kix returned to his bus. "So," he said with a devilish grin, "she likes balloons, does she?"

Kix and Ronnie moved quickly. They snuck up behind Jo Dee, blindfolded her and whisked her to where their *B&D* hot air balloon was ready for take-off. She was airborne before she knew where she was or what was happening.

"Man, did she squeal!" Kix said. "I guess she's afraid of heights."

Suddenly, the balloon started descending rapidly. It even brushed a few treetops. Onlookers watching from the ground, suspecting they were about to witness an accident, called the fire department. Some extremely stern fire officials met the group when they landed. Kix explained that it was all a trick to scare Jo Dee, but the officials remained stonefaced.

Then he tried a different avenue. "Do y'all like hillbilly music?"

From the beginning, Brooks & Dunn have been almost as well-known for their stage set up, specifically the stuff on the stage, as for the performance of their hit songs.

"We call it our redneck fun factor," Kix said.

"The more the better," Ronnie said.

Disco ball-mirrored; whirling longhorn heads; fiery explosions; a smoke-belching leaf-blower disguised to look like a flame-throwing guitar; cannons blasting 120 pounds of multi-colored confetti; huge video screens blasting images of stampeding cattle and race cars; airport landing lights. These are the guys who use the same set designers as the Rolling Stones and Z.Z. Top. Not exactly an understated, demure duo.

Perhaps B&D's best-known stage props are their huge, inflatable, Pink Floyd-style balloons. The huge *Boot Scoot* boot. The 15-foot-tall Rock My World Girls. And, of course, their legendary steerhead, "Bubba."

The night of the 1996 ACM Awards was to be Bubba's last stand. After several years of being inflated, deflated, and tossed into a semi-truck night after night, Bubba was full of holes. At the rehearsal for their performance of "My Maria" for that night's show, Dick Clark, whose production company put on the awards show, approached Dony Wynn, B&D's touring drummer from 1995-1999. Clark told Dony they wanted to deflate "Bubba" and have him collapse across him at the end of the song. Dony figured, *"Why not?"*

The production people, who wanted the stunt to be a surprise, cleared the building of everyone but the B&D band. They ran through the song twice.

"It's all about getting out there and having fun. You don't go to a concert to get bummed out or depressed."

– Ronnie

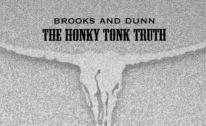

Do the huge mirrored steerheads hanging
on each side of the set have names?
"Yeah," Kix says. "The one on the right is Bob."
And the one on the left?
"Bob"

"The first time it comes down," Dony said, "it's not too bad. Nothing really happens. It kind of falls across me, drapes over my cymbals, and catches them. But Bubba was a huge, three-story-tall, Macy's parade kind of thing. The second time, he comes down hard, bending my cymbal stands. His two horns knocked Danny [Milliner] and Tony [King] over. Knocked me off my stool. We weren't hurt, just startled. We all said, well, if that's the worst it could be, then we're fine with it."

Several hours later, it was showtime. Dony heard the stage manager counting down, 30, 25, 20... then he heard B&D's tour manager, Scott Edwards, scream, "Cut it! Cut it!" The stage manager screamed back, "No! Dick wants it! ...15, 14, 13..." Scotty again, "Cut it! Cut it!" Dony knew there was something wrong (evidently Bubba had taken on air), but he didn't know what to do. The show was live. Kix and Ronnie were out front. The band began to play.

"We start, and I see this huge shadow flying all around me," Dony said. "Then, the audience goes completely bug-eyed. The thing comes down around us. People are laughing, screaming..."

Dony said after he crawled out from under the hulking Bubba, he noticed the crowd still reeling from Clark's "surprise," which later made its way to Dick Clark's *TV's Bloopers and Practical Jokes* show.

"But then," he said, "I looked in the front row and noticed one person was quiet and stone-faced. It was Garth [Brooks]. Perhaps Jeff Foxworthy, the next presenter, said it best: "You know you're a redneck when your bull's head falls on your drummer."

Brooks & Dunn won the award for Entertainer of the Year that night.

"A fitting tribute to Bubba," Dony said.

Only 45 minutes prior to showtime, Ronnie, wearing cut-off jean shorts, was calmly sitting Indian style at the table in his bus eating steak. His then four-year-old daughter, Haley, was crawling through his legs. She hoisted herself up onto his lap to show him where she just stubbed her toe. He and his family had just returned from a day trip to Disney World that he described as "a hoot." He said a couple of years ago, he would never have even considered riding roller coasters only hours before a show.

"Man," he said, rubbing Haley's toe, "I used to be so bad! The bus was my prison. I'd sit there all day and worry about hitting a wrong note."

Sinus problems? Anxiety? Nasal surgery and years of experience have finally assured Ronnie that wrong notes will be the exception. But the early days were a different story. Even in exotic locales,

sometimes Ronnie refused to leave his room or bus until showtime.

Early in their career, *Brooks & Dunn* went to Switzerland to play a country music festival with *Little Texas* and several other acts.

"We took an all-night flight and I had a sinus infection," Ronnie said. "I felt awful. And this guy Rusty Wier, an old songwriter guy from Austin, sat up smoking his cigarettes all night long. He kept his cigarette in his hand. I just watched him all night. I'd wake up, look over, and the smoke would go right under my nose."

Even feeling beat-up from the trip couldn't keep Ronnie from appreciating the scenery. For a few minutes anyway.

"It was unreal!" Ronnie said. "We flew into Zurich and got into this glass-topped tourist bus. They took us back into the mountains, which I guess was two, maybe three hours back into the most beautiful Alps. It was like a postcard! They put us in this chalet hotel in the town. It opened up into this meadow with a waterfall. I mean *beautiful!* And there was a little stone church that looked like it came out of *Braveheart*. Unbelievable. The train would come through the town at night with that European whistle..."

"It's a good thing he saw it on the way in," Kix said, "because that's about all he saw. I mean we'd check him out at dinner or something, but Ronnie wouldn't leave his hotel room. He was just being a fuddy-duddy. The rest of us were out climbing mountains, riding gondolas..."

The festival lasted several days. Both Kix and Ronnie said it was one of the wildest things they ever saw, with hundreds of Swiss and Germans doing their own version of the American cowboy thing.

"It was the blue one that got me."
—Ronnie

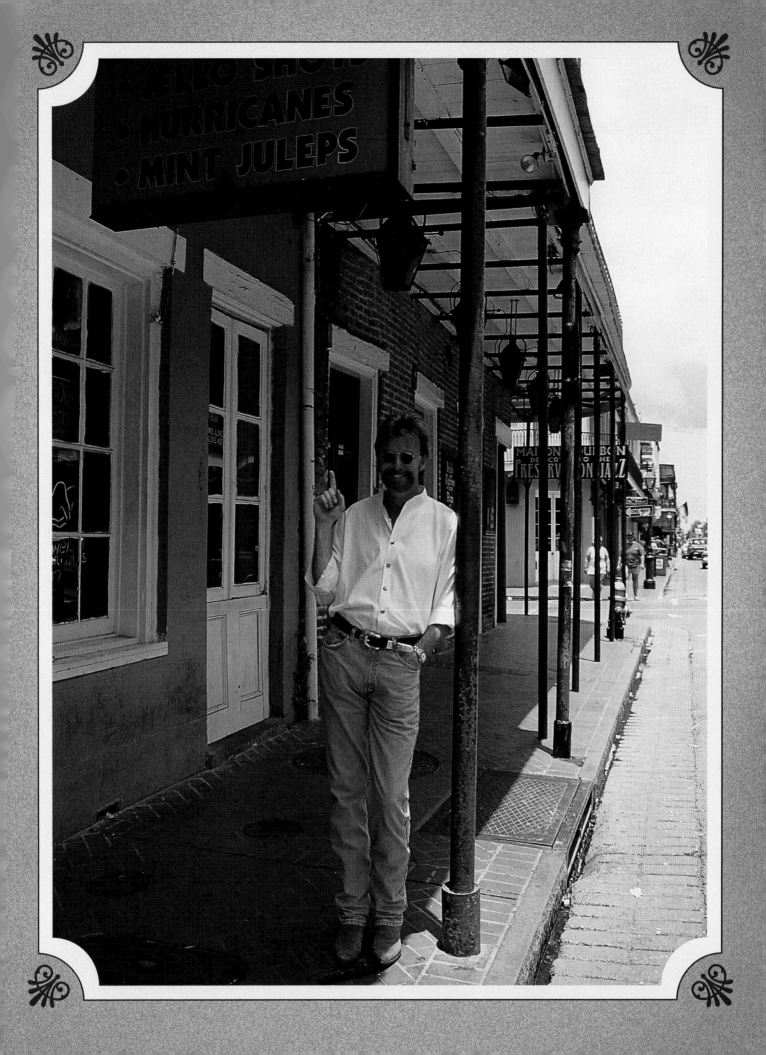

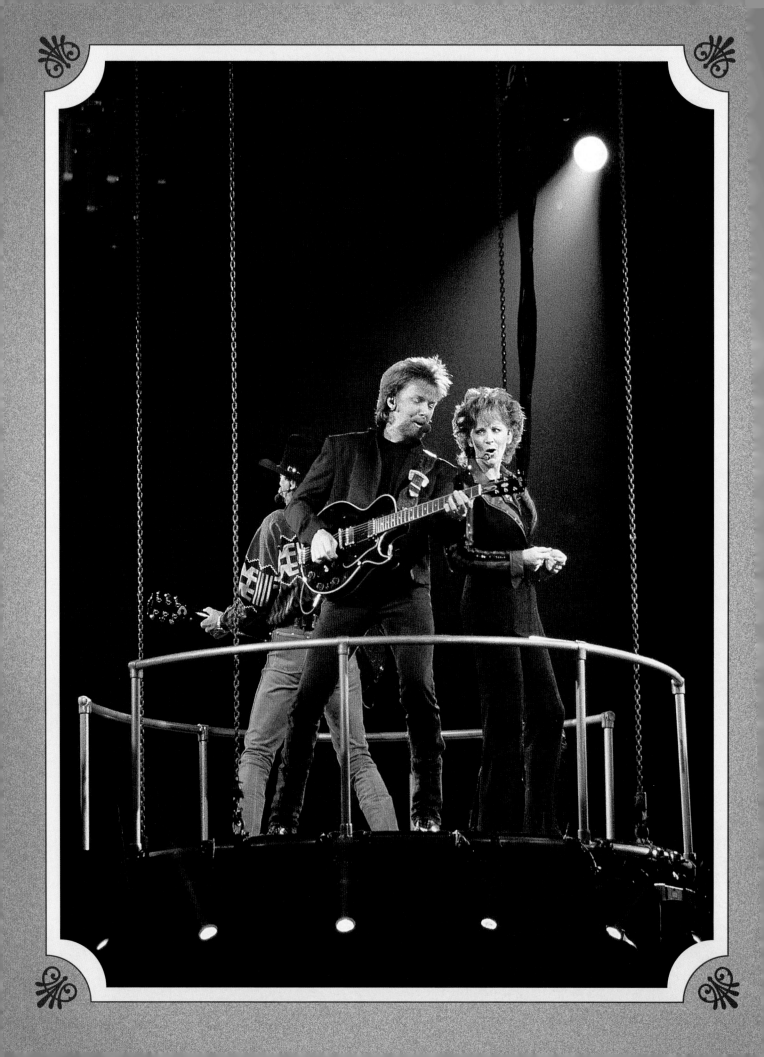

"It was like a beerfest in this huge tent," Ronnie said. "They were all dressed in these sheep wool chaps and they had cowboy pistols. They are looped! Standing on the tables. Rocking. For days!"

"As soon as we started playing, they all got up on top of the picnic tables and started jumping up and down and screaming as loud as they could," Kix said. "It was the craziest thing. They had real guns and stuff. They'd shoot their guns up in the air. It was just pandemonium and the weirdest thing you've ever seen."

One night, the *B&D* bunch went out to dinner. Ronnie stayed at the hotel alone, as usual. While they were gone, however, he decided to pull a prank. Road manager Eric Shinault was his chosen victim.

"If you walk up behind Eric and say, 'Boo!'," Kix explained, "he's just one of these guys who will scream for ten minutes. Like a girl at a Beatles concert. So while we were gone, Ronnie went and got under Eric's bed in the dark — their balconies connected and Eric left his back door open. And Eric came in and got in bed and Ronnie crawled out and 'Aaaaaaaaaaaaah!' You could hear it all over the hotel. We all came running out of our rooms to find out who was getting stabbed. Ronnie was under there for a long time — hours maybe. And it just made his whole life."

Kix said that was "a good one," but one of his all time favorite memories of Ronnie came at the end of the trip.

"We were leaving to go to the airport and Ronnie goes, 'Wait!' He bought a box camera and stood in the middle of the street in that little Swiss village and did a 360, snapping pictures. He snapped a whole roll of film just turning a circle in one place. Then he said, 'Let's go.' Ha! Those were the pictures of his trip!"

During B&D's second joint tour with Reba McEntire in 1998, there came a point in Reba's show every night when she would leave the stage while her band kept playing. The audience was treated to a huge surprise when a few minutes later, Reba appeared on a small stage in the back of the auditorium singing Aretha Franklin's "Respect."

The stunt looked high-tech, as if Reba had been shot through a magic chute to rise from the other stage. But in reality, the trick was pulled-off in a very low-tech manner. While the band played, Reba hopped into a laundry cart-sized black box, crunched herself into a ball and was wheeled by a stagehand to the back of the room. She then climbed out and stepped onto the stage before anyone missed her.

Ronnie and Kix had their eye on Reba's box from day one.

"One night," Kix said, "I just hopped in it and waited for her. Of course she's so methodical. She comes offstage and plops down right on top of me. I went *aaaahhh!*

"To me, B & D are the country ZZ Top. Right when I started they told me, we want you hanging 10 out there. I loved it. They were gracious with the spotlight...still are. That's pretty uncommon to put band members up front."

—guitar player Charlie Crowe

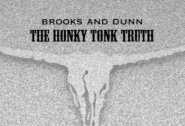

"'Whiskey Under the Bridge' and 'My Next Broken Heart' are easy to confuse. They're both shuffles that have the same kind of lead-in. One night, the band played 'Whiskey' and Ronnie sang 'My Next Broken Heart.' By the middle of the song, Ronnie was in the stratosphere! So high! But I like stuff like that. I think it's interesting to see where it's gonna land. I think it's funny. But then Kix says to me, 'Funny for who?' Because he's the one who has to get out of it!"

—*keyboard player Dwain Rowe*

She shouted, '*Get out of my box!*' We all thought it was funny, but Narvel (her husband and manager) put a guard on the box after that."

"Well, the guy who was picked to guard the box was also the guy who went out and got girls to dance to "Mama Don't Get Dressed Up for Nothing" in front of the stage. One night he got a bunch of strippers and got them to dance. They were pulling their tops up and the camera guys were covering them topless on the big screens. Narvel fired him."

"So he's been fired but he's still the guard. That's the night we planned to put the stink bomb in her box. Since he's fired, he's like, do whatever you want. Then Reba's fixin' to come off and this thing's [the stink bomb] in a glass capsule. Ronnie's trying to break it but he can't. So I took off to get something to break it with; I was gonna get a hammer or something but there was a towel there. Ronnie just took the towel, wrapped it around it, and stomped on it. He goes, "I got it! I got it!" and I started coming back. I'm like halfway back and it hit me right in the Adam's apple. It makes you want to puke. It's like rotten eggs but it makes you want to throw up. Really bad. So he takes the towel and throws it in there."

"Reba jumps in , closes the door, and takes off. The last thing I see is this red head sticking up through a hole in the top and her turning to the side just trying to get a breath. Like a turkey shoot! You know, when the turkey sticks its head up they try to shoot its head off?"

"So me and Ronnie looked at each other and went, 'Oh, man. She looks hot.' We're waiting for her to come up on "Respect," ya know. We wait and she comes up. She's got this look on her face like she's just thrown up or she needs to, and she goes (muffled, with gritted teeth) R E S P E C T... like, I'm gonna kill you guys. And she does the song, and gets through it being the consummate professional that she is. But she is really mad now."

"So she's walking through the audience making her way to the stage and here's this guy who had just gotten two beers. He didn't realize that Reba's walking down the aisle. His wife taps him on the shoulder and points. He turns around and slings his beers on Reba. So now she's like sloshing and she's red-faced. You can see, everybody that wants to kind of go up and touch her, they back off as soon as they smell... well, she's got this stink on her so bad."

"Then we gotta do the encore. That night our buses were parked across the street. They had a van down there for us to go across the street to our buses. We did the encore... she's kind of half-smiling like, it's OK, everything's fine. She had a few minutes to get it together and figure out how she was gonna retaliate... and she will retaliate. I'm thinking, the whole way through the encore... I'm not getting in that van. I don't know what's gonna happen, but I'm not getting in there. As soon as the song ended, I jumped off the side of the stage like John Wilkes Booth and took off running all the way up the tunnel, all the way across the street as fast as I could, and got on my bus and locked the door."

"Kix falls all the time. He gets overly excited when he first goes on stage. He likes to push me when we go on, then a few more times throughout the show. He thinks it makes us look like buddies. It's irritating from time to time, and distracting . . . but he thinks it looks like we've bonded or something."

—Ronnie

Brooks & Dunn were playing the Las Vegas Hilton in late 2000, the site of Elvis' famed concerts. In honor of the King, Ronnie sang "Blue Christmas." With a hand-lettered cue card in full view, he sat on a stool next to Kix and started belting out the tune.

In the middle of the song, Kix left the stage and returned holding a rhinestone-studded Elvis cape. He draped it around Ronnie's shoulders. Ronnie gave him a smirk, then tossed the cape into the audience.

Production manager Randy "Baja" Fletcher gasped, "Oh god! That really is Elvis' cape." They had gotten the Hilton people to take it out of the vault. The next night, Ronnie sang "Blue Christmas" again, but this time, Kix did not put a cape around Ronnie's shoulders.

"We're no longer allowed to touch Elvis' things," Kix explains.

When the new President is a Texan, it's no surprise when *Brooks & Dunn* are invited to play the inauguration.

"I never thought I was the sentimental, patriotic type," Ronnie says. "But when the President-elect, his wife, and the Cheneys made their entrance at the top of the Lincoln Memorial steps, I was completely overcome with emotion. The entire armed forces color guard was in formation down the Lincoln Memorial steps. As Sandi Patti sang 'The National Anthem' and wave after wave of jets and helicopters flew over, I looked out over the reflecting pool towards the Washington Memorial and the Capitol

in awe and disbelief. I had to fight back tears for several minutes thinking that I might not be able to get through our song!"

"Kix and I were on opposite sides of the stage awaiting our introduction by Larry King. The Bushes and the entire staff were seated right next to me — I had to walk through them to get out on stage. We played "Only In America," a song on the new CD. It's about having the freedom to pursue your dreams. I glanced over towards their seating area and Mr. Bush gave me a very "Presidential" thumbs up."

"Backstage we met Muhammad Ali and Wayne Newton. The secret service escort informed us to follow them for the Grand Finale. Our guitar player, Charlie, my daughter Whitney, Kix and I went out on-stage. I felt someone move over next to me. It was Colin Powell! He politely introduced himself.

"Then Whitney exploded, "Oh God, Dad, here he comes!" I of course thought she meant the President, but it was Ricky Martin. She shoved a camera in my hand, bounded right past Mr. Bush, and took her place beside Ricky and shouted, "TAKE MY PICTURE DAD !" Even the secretary of state chuckled as I held the camera over my head trying to get a shot... I failed... But luckily our guitarist Charlie Crowe caught her on video."

"Afterwards, Mr. Bush asked Kix and I where we were from... I said I had attended grade school in Midland, Texas, for a short while and that I was a Texas native. Kix followed by saying that he was from Shreveport, Louisiana...*East Texas*. Brown noser!"

Viva Las Vegas — *"We're no longer allowed to touch Elvis' things."*

HILLBILLY SONGS

Brand New Truck

In June of 1991, *Brooks & Dunn* were several weeks into their first tour when their first single, "Brand New Man," was released. The record climbed the charts fast, then held for several weeks at number six.

During a plane ride both Ronnie and Kix say they will never forget, the stewardess came over the loud-speaker and said, "Mr. Ronnie Dunn, please report to the front of the plane immediately."

Ronnie popped out of his seat wide-eyed saying, "What'd I do?"

"He goes up," Kix continued, "and the stewardess goes, 'Your wife called. Something about... you owe her a truck?'"

Ronnie went numb. The first time his wife Janine heard the demo of "Brand New Man," she bet him a new truck that it would go to number one. Ronnie knew what the message meant; he just couldn't believe it. When the plane landed, he and Kix bolted to the airport payphone to see if it could be true. It was. "Brand New Man" was number one. Janine Dunn went to test drive a Ford Explorer the next day.

"These boys are single-handedly keeping country music alive."
—David Letterman

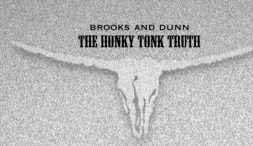

Scootin' the Boot

The next three singles *B&D* released off their *Brand New Man* album ("My Next Broken Heart," "Neon Moon" and "Boot Scootin' Boogie") all shot to number one. This was astonishing enough. But the fourth single, "Boot Scootin' Boogie" was exceptional not just because it was the fourth consecutive number one from a debut band, but because a funny thing happened on the way up the charts. "Boot Scootin' Boogie" started a whole... *thing*.

"I wasn't thinking genre when I wrote it," Ronnie said. "I didn't write it as a dance. I was trying to be metaphorical. 'Boot Scootin' Boogie' was a lifestyle. Real light and trite on purpose. When they turned it into a dance, well... that's not what I wrote the song about. 'Boot Scootin' Boogie' is a lifestyle... how people come out, do their deal on the weekends. Then the linedance... I was like, don't sugarcoat it. It's bad enough."

"Boot Scootin' Boogie's" origin can be traced to an Abilene Texas parking lot in the early 70s. A fellow-musician told Ronnie, "Yeah, we're playing a 'boot scoot' down in Sanford."

"A *boot scoot*," Ronnie thought. "What a great term!" He tucked it away and retrieved it 15 years later.

After "Boot Scoot," the single, came the extended dance mix.

"I had been thinking about putting together two different styles of music just to see what would happen," producer Scott Hendricks said. "My original thought was to put bluegrass behind a real hard-driving, bass kind of sound. Imagine taking Peter Gabriel's 'So' and stripping everything away, except the drums and the bass, and putting bluegrass on top of that."

"I thought maybe this would work with 'Boot Scoot.' So I called this big-time programmer/producer who recommended Brian Tankersley."

After working on the song for one week, Brian met Scott in Brentwood, Tennessee, to play the tape.

"He played me 'Boot Scootin' Boogie' with kind of a dance thing," Scott said. "I thought it was incredible. Radically different. Nobody had ever heard anything close to that. Ronnie and Kix liked it. I give them a lot of credit because they were trying it."

Scott then played the tape for Arista staff members.

"They flipped out over this one lick before it was even through the first chorus," Scott says. "Everyone pretty much said it was awesome."

So, encouraged by his staff, Scott played it for Tim DuBois.

Scott was disappointed by Tim's reaction, ("What is that?") and by the response from "another person" in the room who said, "It'll never sell."

But Arista staffers and Scott kept pushing. Scott asked Tim to give him money to push the record. He agreed and Arista released the very first country music dance mix. So "Boot Scootin' Boogie," combined with the popularity of another hit, Billy Ray Cyrus' "Achy Breaky Heart," ignited the line dance craze of the early 1990s.

Kix says there's always a psycho drama before deciding which audience member he'll dance with during "Boot Scootin' Boogie": "If you get somebody that's too out of control when you jump down there, all they can do is jump up and down and have a fit. So you don't want them. You want somebody who's at least half in their foot."

"Sometimes Ronnie just doesn't want to hold a guitar, so playing the cowbell is something for him to do. One time, he broke a drumstick and goes, 'Hey! I need a drumstick!' So I threw it to him. And he threw it out into the audience. Now he'll throw as many as 50 or 60 a night. We've had no major lawsuits yet. One time at a show in Nashville it did put a knot on a girl's head pretty bad. But we pulled her backstage and gave her autographs, smoothed it over. She wasn't permanently damaged though."

—guitar tech Jeff Kersey

*"We were playing with Alabama in San Francisco, and there was a long ramp down
and another ramp going up in the middle of the floor onto the stage. The lights were out,
the intro was starting, and Kix went running down the stage. It was a black floor and he
didn't see where the angle on the ramps changed. Kix basically ran into the floor and he
rolled onto the stage. He was running so fast that he flipped, knocked his hat off,
his guitar went flying, and I swear to you, no one in the audience even saw.
He landed on his feet, put on his hat, and started to play. I turned to the guys in the
band and said, 'Did you see that?' That's pretty wild stuff."*

—Ronnie

"That started it," Scott said. "Whether we want to be given credit for it or not, I don't know at this point. Like everything else, it ran its course. But it was definitely a rocket engine on the back of this album."

Before a show one night, during the time "Boot Scootin' Boogie" was hogging the number one spot, Ronnie bought a T-shirt that said, "Real Men Don't Line Dance." Giggling, he showed it to Kix who promptly suggested he burn it.

"What's really funny is it was hard to think of it as a craze or a fad, because I'd been watching people line dance in clubs in Oklahoma and Texas for years," Ronnie laughed. "It's nothing new. It's been going on since Bob Wills! I think the 'craze' was more about the rising popularity of country music at the time the song came out."

"When we released the dance mix, I felt like a little kid who threw a rock through a window and then ran and hid in the bushes and waited to see what happens."

B&D considered playing the dance version in concert. Kix said they rehearsed it, but it was a definite thumbs down.

"We sounded like B&D and the Sunshine Band!" Ronnie said.

Years later, *Brooks & Dunn* still play "Boot Scootin' Boogie," the non-dance version, at every show. Kix, who swears neither he nor Ronnie know any line dances, usually picks a dance partner out of the first couple of rows halfway through the song and gives her an impromptu twirl. The big moment has only flopped once.

"After going through all the bars in America and never having a slip-up we played the *New Faces* show at a radio seminar. It's a real big deal when you showcase for all the radio stations the first time. I jumped off the stage and this girl would not dance with me. I'm going, 'C'mon!' You know, pulling her up. She was like, no. So I turned to a girl at the next table and she wouldn't either. It was horrible. By the time I got a 'taker' the song was over."

"Most of the inspiration for writing songs comes from life, like 'Little Miss Honky Tonk.' That came from playing rodeos and fairs in the Midwest and seeing all the little rodeo queens going around with their sashes. Ya know, Little Miss Junior Rodeo, Little Miss Saddle Soap. The best songs come from real stuff. After seeing those gals I sat down and tried to come up with something unique."

—Ronnie

In the Studio

In Nashville, the musicians who play in shows are usually different than those who play on records. Brent Mason is an A-list studio guitar player who has played on records for almost every major country act including Alan Jackson, Trisha Yearwood, George Strait, Shania Twain and *Brooks & Dunn.*

"The first song I worked on with *B&D* was 'Cool Drink of Water,' I think," Brent says. "Before Dwight Yoakam came along, things had been smooth. But *B&D* wanted a rough, edgy, roadhouse kind of thing, so they asked me to throw the amps up to get a 'live bandy' sound. It was different because most others liked to work directly through the boards, no amps, because it made for a clean sound. But Ronnie and Kix wanted kick-butt, roadhouse, loud country music. Boot-scoot dance hall kind of stuff. I knew there was something to it. It was great, not contrived at all."

Rob Hajacos, another A-list session player (Garth, Shania, George Strait), created the distinctive fiddle hooks on many of B&D's records.

"I remember early on telling Ronnie that I was blown away with how they just let us play and be ourselves on stuff like 'Neon Moon' and 'Boot Scootin' Boogie,'" Rob says. "The result was that their sound defined an era of music. It was guitar-heavy, but to use the term 'country rock' with them would be slanderous. Their music is unto itself. It's that simple."

"They started a new wave of country music," Brent says. "All of a sudden everybody tried to sound like them. But it's hard — they have a very distinct sound. They're vocals are distinct; you know who it is. You can tell Ronnie's voice and Kix's voice on the radio right away. After they started, in other sessions people were constantly asking for 'the B&D sound.' All the labels were trying to find the new *Brooks & Dunn.* Nobody ever could."

"We work fast and off-the-cuff in the studio," Brent Mason says. "Playing with them in the studio is like being in a bar band. It's very conducive to creating music. It's easy to come up with things. No one gets too analytical. There's no second-guessing. It just keeps rolling."

Not all country music acts work this way. For instance, Brent says that Shania Twain's producer, Mutt Lange, is very precise and exacting when he works.

"He's very unpretentious and not intimidating, but it's more pressure because it's intense," Brent says. "Mutt plans productions a year in advance and lays out exactly what he wants you to do. He'll take a lot of time to get it right. Like, one time, we worked on an intro for three hours. There's not too much spontaneity. I feel more like a machine."

During B&D sessions, Brent says, they always seem to get on a roll.

"Studio musicians get bored easily," he says. "So I think it's better to get a song in the first couple of takes. Because you can feel it; the emotion and excitement is there."

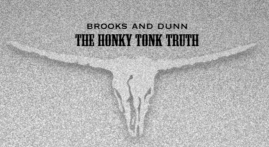

"Husbands & Wives"

"Cutting that was just a whim," Ronnie says. "I was in the studio, and we had a little bit of down time, and I looked at [Don] Cook and said, 'Do you remember that Roger Miller song? Does anybody know the lyrics? I want to cut it while we have a minute.' So he called Sony, and they faxed the lyrics over and we cut it. And it just worked. After one take everyone just looked at each other like, 'Whoa, this sounds great.' Everything is typically so methodical and clinical. With this song it just happened, and that's really a great feeling."

"It was the 1998 Country Music Awards," says drummer Dony Wynn. "Country music's going through all this pop and stuff. And we were doing a Roger Miller tune, 'Husbands & Wives,' a brilliant tale that harkens back to an older, simpler time. So Kris Kristofferson is sitting in the front row. He's one of the old school. A great writer. We're doing the song and he is just digging it. Whistling, fingers in the mouth. On his feet! Doing this song shows there are a lot of levels to B&D. That's part of their success."

"I don't want us just to be the proverbial shit-howdy show out there on the road."

—Ronnie

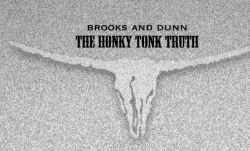

"You'll Always Be Loved By Me"

"We were in Lake Tahoe, playing Caesar's," Ronnie says. "The first thing they told me was, 'We're putting you in the Tom Jones Suite.' I said, 'Cool! All right!' I expected women to be knocking on the door all night. We were up there goofing off, and once again, it was 3 am. These songs seem to come up around that time. We just popped it out from a hook that Terry (McBride) had. We didn't realize we had a song until the next day when we went back and looked at it."

"See Jane Dance"

"See Jane Dance" was written by Charlie Crowe, the lead-guitar player in B&D's touring band. It got its start one early summer afternoon in Charlie's back-yard hot tub. He was sitting in the tub recovering from a root canal with the help of "those special pills they give you" and a couple of cold beers.

"I wasn't trying to do anything particular when I wrote this," Charlie says. "I was just writing to entertain myself."

While he was writing, his wife Kim, who was six months pregnant with their first child, came outside to join him.

"In a couple of months all your inspiration will be coming from books like Spot and Jane," Kim teased. "You'll be singing, See Jane Run, daddy!"

Laughing, Charlie got out of the tub, toweled off and put down a riff, changing 'See Jane Run' to 'See Jane Dance.' Then, he recorded it on his new home studio equipment.

"I really don't sing," Charlie says. "But I just started hollering into the mike anyway, just to get it down."

After several re-writes and several more demos cut by *Brooks & Dunn*, the song made its way to their *Steers & Stripes* album despite the line in the chorus about "leopard underpants.".

"Well, what else rhymes with dance?" Charlie says.

"Only in America"

Backstage at the Las Vegas Hilton in December, 2000. In their dressing room, Kix and Ronnie were sitting around before their last show of the year.

Ronnie was slouched in his chair with his legs stretched way out in front of him, and Kix was sitting leaning on the opposite end of the couch dressed in his bright blue stage shirt and pressed Wranglers, loudly strumming his guitar.

His black hat was sitting next to him on the table, "inside up" for good luck. He strummed away, first humming, then singing a song he and frequent co-writing partner Don Cook recently finished. "Mmmmmmmmm....Only in America...

"I like it," Ronnie said. "I like the hook: barmp, barrrrrowwwww, barmp, barrrrowwwww. You could maybe change that one thing dum dum dawooon... I like it. I think it's a winner. This kind of song..."

"I know!" Kix said. "And it's a good time to rally the country, ya know?"

"I'm with ya, buddy!" Ronnie said. "I think it's perfect. Barmp, barmp, badadad-um da da dum... just, ya know, stab the snot out of it!"

Kix cracked up.

"It'll do in a pinch!" Ronnie said. "Maybe in that one line you should change the word to "changed" instead of..."

Kix changed the subject to chide Ronnie about his special performance of the Elvis song, "Blue Christmas." "Man, you wrote down the words the last two nights and you still screwed it up! Ha!"

A girl in her late twenties came in wearing a backstage pass. She stopped in front of Kix and whispered something.

"Sign your what?" Kix said loudly to rowdy laughter. "Oh! Your *boot!*"

Mmmmmm. Only in America...

"Has anybody noticed that every time Charlie Crowe's
role in the show gets bigger his pants get tighter?"
—anonymous band member

"Kix is just a frustrated actor."

— Ronnie

"South of Santa Fe" video

For the "South of Santa Fe" video, the *Brooks & Dunn* crew traveled to Tucson, Arizona, where Ronnie and Kix got to dress up as cowboys. During the course of the video, Kix is on the run, being chased by Ronnie and his posse. During one scene, Ronnie is supposed to crouch near some prickly pear cacti, feel the ground for freshly-spritzed fake blood, and look into the distance. His line is, "He can't be far . . . this blood's still fresh." Then he is supposed to mount his horse and ride off.

Take 1: Ronnie crouches near the cacti, feels the ground, and looks into the distance. "He can't be far . . . this blood's still fresh." He strides to his horse, puts a foot in the stirrup, and halfway up, one long leg dangling behind him, the horse takes off.

Take 2: Ronnie crouches, feels the ground, looks into the distance, "He can't be far . . ." but all that can be heard is his horse loudly munching on grass, muffling out his line.

Take 3: Ronnie crouches, feels the ground, looks into the distance, " . . .this blood's still fresh." Ronnie's dramatic stare is replaced by a look of fright and disgust as he feels his horse's nose on the back of his neck. "Is there a horse loogie on my head?"

Take 4: Ronnie crouches, feels the ground, says his line, and manages finally to mount the horse.

"Lost and Found" video

Brooks & Dunn strayed far from home to film the video for their fifth single, "Lost and Found." Location: Tijuana, Mexico. This song, which Kix wrote with Don Cook before he met Ronnie, is full of imagery of a dusty, rough-and-tumble border town. Mike Merriman, who directed the first four B&D videos, says for "Lost and Found," gritty Tijuana was the first place that came to mind. Dealing with The Mexican Film Counsel turned out to be a bit sticky though.

"We contacted them for permission to film in Mexico," Merriman says, "They wrote back saying they would grant permission only if we portrayed their country in a positive light. Well, Tijuana is Tijuana, but we promised we would do our best. Then they said we had to use Mexican actors to portray Ronnie and Kix!"

Merriman, a mellow-mannered guy, patiently convinced his contacts at The Mexican Film Counsel that a *Brooks &* *Dunn* video would be better if it did, in fact, feature Brooks and Dunn.

"After we paid the fee they let us bring the real deal," Merriman says.

"Rock the Whole World"

After *Brooks & Dunn* made the video for "Rock My World," they recorded introductions in several different languages (Japanese, Portuguese, Italian) so the video could be marketed internationally.

"They had tutors from the Berlitz class," Ronnie explained. "They'd coach us real quick with cue cards."

"But we didn't have a clue what we were saying," Kix laughed. "My dad was with some friends in a bar in Italy. They were watching TV and Ronnie and I came on. We thought we said, 'Here's our new Rock My World video', in Italian, but everybody in that bar stopped and burst into laughter. So there's no telling what we said."

"Their music seems light sometimes, with funny lyrics and all…
But really, it's Hillbilly Poetry."
— fiddle player Rob Hajacos

*The Butch Cassidy and
Sundance Kid of country music.*

THIS
BROOKS & DUNN
THING

IT ALL BEGAN in Spring 1992 when *Brooks & Dunn* won two Academy of Country Music (ACM) Awards for *Top Vocal Duet* and *Top New Vocal Duet or Group*.

"What I remember more than anything was trying to keep from crying," Ronnie said. "I mean, I'm a guy! We're both guys. Oh man, no way! When we got backstage we couldn't even look at each other... we had to look away."

It became easier and easier not to cry as the years passed and *Brooks & Dunn* piled on the awards. They made the duo category their own, winning it every year from 1992-2000 (ACM's) and 1992-1999 (the Country Music Association).

Also crowding the tops of Ronnie and Kix's respective fireplaces: a slew of other trophies including the big Kahuna, *Entertainer of the Year*. *B&D* have taken it home three times, twice from the ACM, and once from the CMA.

The first time they won *Entertainer of the Year* at the ACM Awards in 1995, it was Jay Leno who came to the podium to announce the winner. Kix said Leno opened the envelope, paused, then nodded his head and said, "Yeah, that's what I thought..."

"When he said that," Kix said, "I thought for sure it was Garth... or Strait. Then he goes, 'Brooks & Dunn!'"

Kix said his only thought as he made his way up to the stage was, "I can't believe Leno thought we were gonna win."

After accepting the award, he and Ronnie gave each other high fives and hugs. Kix said it was one the few times he and Ronnie openly expressed any emotion towards each other. Mostly though, he said, they kept looking at each other and saying, "Do you believe this stuff?"

"We really felt like we had gotten to the top of Everest that night," Kix said. "I mean I was shocked. I really was."

Several months later, Brooks & Dunn went on to win *Entertainer of the Year* at the CMA Awards as well, beating out fellow nominees George Strait, Alan Jackson, Garth Brooks, and Vince Gill. The following Spring, they again won *Entertainer of the Year* at the ACMs.

"That was even more of a shock than the first time!" Kix said.

After winning their third *Entertainer of the Year* award, a backstage reporter asked Kix to explain the reason for their success.

"If we knew the answer to that, we would have screwed it up a long time ago."

"Kix and I have come to terms with a lot of differences that we had — our tastes in music and our personalities or whatever," Ronnie said. "We used to hold back. When you don't really know someone all that well, you do that. I mean, we were thrown together in this partnership and it took off like a rocket ship headed for the moon. Then, we had to get to know one another. It is, in a lot of ways, like a marriage — the way you relate to each other. Honesty has a lot to do with it. And the better you know someone, the more apt you are to be honest, drop your guard and come clean. A lot of times you'll go along with something you don't want to do just because you don't want to stir something up or you don't know how they're going to react. Now, we just get things out on the table."

"It's just like any friendship or relationship," Kix said. "You either learn too much about each other and you get burned out, and you go your separate ways, or you find out things that you can live with. Basically, it comes down to being comfortable with each other. With guys like us, it could have easily gone either way. We're both pretty independent-minded in general. But we don't have any problems, and all along we've been feeling that part of our relationship out."

"Despite what you've read in the *Star*," Kix said, "We're gonna keep playing and making music as long as you want us to."

"We're not a mother-daughter team."

Brooks & Dunn

American Music Awards
Favorite Country Band, Duo or Group
—1997, 2000

Country Music Association (CMA)
Entertainer of the Year — 1996

Academy of Country Music (ACM)
Entertainer of the Year — 1995, 1996

Duo of the Year (CMA) and *Top Vocal Duet* (ACM)
Winners eight consecutive years

Best Country Group
Playboy's Reader Music Poll

Grammy Award:
Best Country Performance, Duo or Group with Vocal
("Hard Working Man," "My Maria")

17 Number One Singles:
Brand New Man
Boot Scootin' Boogie
That Ain't No Way To Go
You're Gonna Miss Me
    When I'm Gone
A Man This Lonely
My Next Broken Heart
We'll Burn That Bridge
Little Miss Honk Tonk
My Maria
He's Got You
Neon Moon
She Used To Be Mine
She's Not The Cheatin' Kind
I Am That Man
If You See Him/If You See Her
How Long Gone
Husbands & Wives

Brooks & Dunn Tours:
Mootalica
Electric Rodeo
Steel Canyon
Concrete Rodeo
Asphalt Cowboys
Neon Circus and Wild West Show